WALKING BUTTERFLY

COMFY COCOON TO FLYING FREE

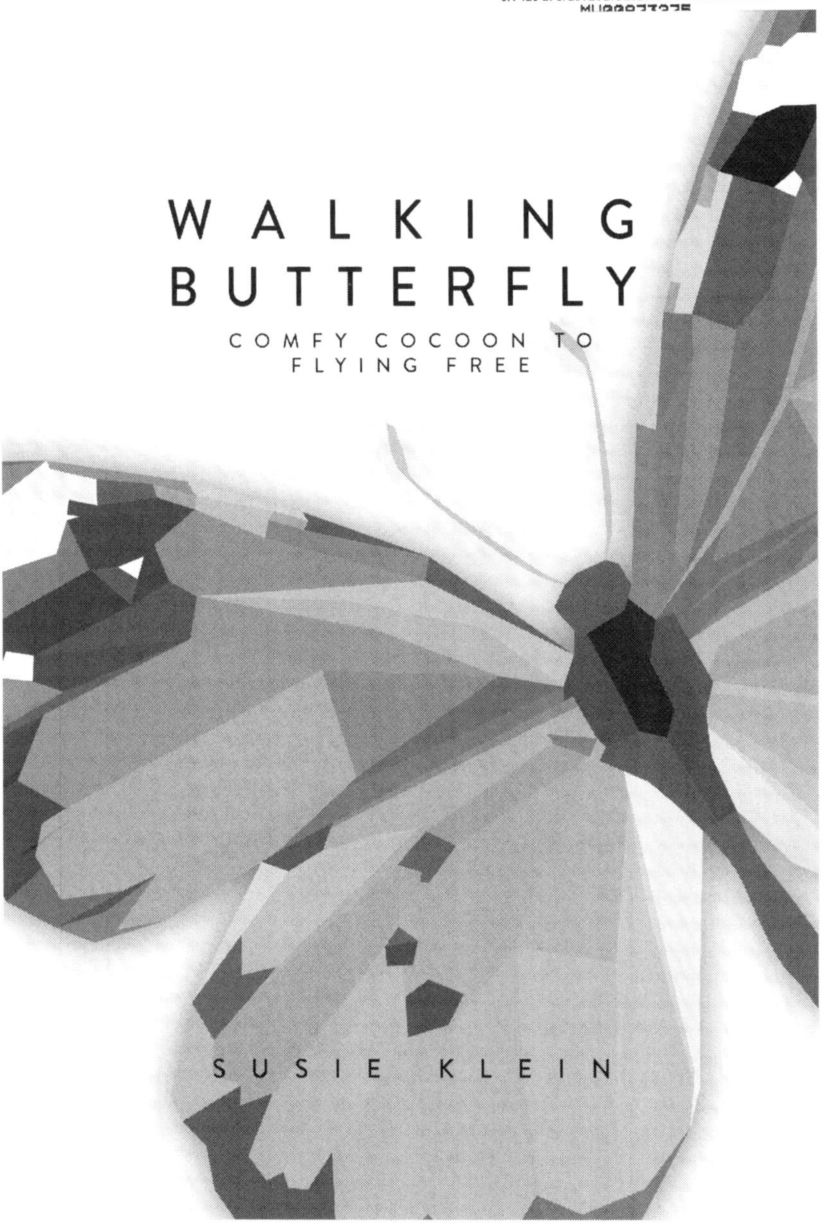

SUSIE KLEIN

www.RecoveringChurchLady.com

Cover Design & Interior Layout : Lorraine Box   PropheticArt@sbcglobal.net

ISBN: 13: 978- 1523617623

TABLE OF CONTENTS

To My Family

who watched it all

Thank you

ENDORSEMENTS

I loved this book! Reading it was like lying on a very warm tropical beach as the gentle surf rolled over and refreshed me. I felt wave after wave of God's love as I followed Susie's accounts of her personal journey with the One who is love.

Susie's down to earth wisdom, gentle encouragement and practical perspective on the mystery of God's love, will draw you into a deeper experience and revelation of God's nature, and your own true identity. I highly recommend this book!

Bob Book
Singer, songwriter, worshiper
www.BobBookMusic.com

For years I watched my dear friend Susie Klein, worship in corners of rooms. While others lifted their hearts to God in more outspoken ways, Susie's worship - her Eucharistic practice, if you will - unfolded quietly as she wrote in her journals. This book is the result of her honest and private conversations with her Best Friend seen through the perspective of time and wisdom. Let her light a candle in an unseen corner of your life.

Joyce Milton
Minister, Teacher

Reading Susie Klein's *Walking Butterfly* is the equivalent of standing with arms outstretched, face upturned and heart wide open under a God shower as the inescapable reality of His love saturates every molecule of your being, suffusing your soul with restored identity. She invites you to join her inside a personal gallery of spiritual snapshots and then leads you on a leisurely stroll down hallways lined with photographs where, much to your surprise, you find images of yourself staring back at you from within the frames. Even if you've imagined God to be good, *Walking Butterfly* will convince you that He's even better than that.

R. G. Ryan
Author

INTRODUCTION

MY HOPE, DESIRE, AND DEAREST wish is that the words you are getting ready to read will feel like a comfortable chat with a friend, about our Great Friend. When sitting together, the best times are those that go deep, don't you think? Surface talk is fine. Talking about movies, books and the people in our lives is an important part of every relationship and I don't see it as a negative way to spend time together at all. But the moments that delve just a bit further under the layers are so satisfying and nurturing to our hearts. Those conversations can include belly laughs, tears and soul-baring truth.

This book has a single message, told over and over again…Because we need to hear this message more than once to get it. It is a message of true love. A love that is bigger, broader and more encompassing than you know. I will attempt to convince you of this ridiculous gift by telling you one story after another describing how God made me a believer in His true love.

Each chapter will begin with a story of a personal encounter between God and me. Then together, we will explore what that may mean for you. The events are not written in chronological order. Feel free to read them in any way you desire. This little book is all about you and how much God loves you. Today, at this moment right now.

The backdrop of the stories you are about to read… slowly, I hope… include over 25 years in full-time ministry in just about every possible church position, from co-pastor to church janitor to founder of a ministry school and many jobs in between. I raised two creative and funny sons and worked alongside my best friend, my husband. God has been the center of my life for as long as I can remember and working for a church was my expression of love to and for Him.

But the stories are not in any way exclusive to ministry-life; you will find hope and meaning in them no matter what your walk in life looks like. He loves what I did, but these short personal stories convinced me that He loves who I am even more than what I do.

My hope, desire and dearest wish is that by the time you close the final page of this book, you will be completely convinced of His love. What better way to spend some time with a friend than to go deep and come back up refreshed in His love?

May you close this book more loved than when you opened it.

Susie Klein

one

WALKING BUTTERFLY

THE BLACK AND WHITE PURSE matched her spectator pumps perfectly and she looked "oh so proper". The pretty butterfly was walking along the sidewalk clutching her handbag in front of her. As a former shoe sales lady, I can tell you that the spectator pump is an ultra conservative classic style of dress shoe. It is distinguished by the two contrasting colors with the heel and toecap always a darker color, almost like a grown-up saddle shoe. A proper lady wore them with a matching purse in the crook of her arm.

This is the picture that God gave me one quiet morning while alone in the sanctuary of the small church where my husband was the pastor. That funny little walking butterfly began a long and traumatic transformation in me, that many years later took me into a tattoo shop where I asked for a permanent butterfly to be inked onto my wrist at the age of 54. Minus the spectator pumps and purse!

But, to get back to the story of how God used a walking butterfly to change my life.

The idea of a butterfly walking along the sidewalk caught me off guard that morning. Just one week earlier, God had spoken to me very clearly through a completely different butterfly picture. He had revealed to me that I was inside a dark and ugly cocoon, but love was setting me free.

It took years for God to convince me that I was loved. He kept saying it again and again. He sent me love notes through people who prayed for me and through songs on the radio. He said it in books that crossed my path and He whispered His love for me straight into my heart in times of prayer.

But I was slow to believe Him. Fear and love do not get along. The two opposite emotions cannot exist in the same space at the same time. At least not peacefully. I was afraid of the world, its speed, its violence, and its laughter at me if I said the wrong thing or dressed the wrong way. Danger lurked everywhere. So much could go wrong on any given day. Worry and fear became a part of Susie, part of my personality and outlook.

Yes, I had loved God all my life, giving my heart to Jesus at a young age. But life in this world still hurts and bad things happen, so I had built a safe cocoon to hide inside and protect myself. My cocoon worked really well for many years. I was serving God, helping people, and taking care of my family. I was comfortable. My cocoon and I were "just fine, thank you very much!" I had designed it myself, so it fit me perfectly. It was the right size and shape for me. I could have stayed inside my crusty little shell forever… as long as I did not grow.

As I write this I realize that you may need a more tangible picture of what life inside a protective cocoon looks like.

I had no strong opinions about life's little things. My favorite color, flavor or clothing style was always open and re-forming according to who was asking. What restaurant to go to or movie to see was an unanswerable question. People-pleasing was my hobby and worry was a full-time job. Most major decisions were fear-based. Which was the safest, easiest and least risky way? Do not ruffle feathers; do not make a scene, ever.

This pattern made close friendship difficult if not impossible. I was too frightened to approach even the friendliest group of people, assuming they would not be interested in me and would consider me a bother. I took no real risks and felt safest by following all the rules carefully. I frustrated my patient husband by even refusing to jaywalk across the street.

And then God began sending me love notes!

It seemed like every time I picked up a book, stood in line to be prayed for at church or turned on the radio, I was hearing a love message from my God. I even got a little annoyed at this repetitious Sunday school level "word from the Lord". I remember being in more than one group setting as we shared the latest messages we had heard from God. My friends were hearing deeply profound instructions that sent them all over the world speaking to nations and transforming hearts and minds. They had seen pictures of large crowds in arenas listening to them or feeding an entire nation of the poor and wounded. While to me, God was simply saying, *"I love you Susie."*

It was a truth I needed to hear, that I needed to believe.

God's message began to reach me. Deep inside my safe little cocoon, a slow but steady change was taking place. I was beginning to believe

I was God's Beloved. Could He really love me completely? Already? As is? If the Maker of the Universe loves me, and is truly pleased when He looks at me, well, that would change everything! If I could actually believe and embrace such a thing, my whole world would be altered.

Little by little my new form grew and expanded until the crusty cocoon began to feel uncomfortable and small. The fear-filled caterpillar was becoming a butterfly. God was no longer content to let me hide inside my self-designed layer of fear.

The Susie He had in mind was much too big and beautiful for a dark and confining little cocoon.

1 John 4:18 says, *There is no fear in love; but perfect love casts out fear, because fear involves torment* (my interpretation of torment is: *worry*) 1 John 4:18 NKJV (New King James Version Spirit Filled Life Bible 1991 Thomas Nelson).

My cocoon was finally broken open and the butterfly had emerged. She was enjoying the new freedom and broad expanse of life outside the fear-based encasement. I laugh now when I recall one of the first big opinions I expressed. It was in a movie theater. As the movie began, the sound company always gave that little demonstration of their big abilities by going from quiet to super loud in our ears and I hated it. This time I said so. *"I HATE that!"* It felt momentous to me, a major breakthrough that had me chuckling as the movie began.

So on that quiet morning in our sanctuary, I was on my knees asking God to please equip me. I wanted to do all the great assignments He had for me. I told Him I needed more wisdom and talent to be what He wanted me to be. I desperately wanted to be that great big, beautiful butterfly.

His answer was simply two little words, *"Walking butterfly"*. I smiled and even giggled as I could immediately see the prim and proper butterfly with matching shoes and purse walking along the sidewalk.

Why did I laugh?

I had been begging God to equip me. I wanted Him to give me what I needed to fly, now that the cocoon was gone. His answer was right there in the picture. The proper butterfly was dragging a pair of gorgeous wings behind her along the sidewalk.

She is already equipped. I am equipped. I have everything I need to please God. I was already pleasing Him!

The full-grown wings were right there behind me.

YOUR TURN

Friend, you are deeply loved by the Creator of The Universe. God knows you well. His love is not blind; He sees it all. And still He loves. The mighty love God has for you is bigger than the wall or cocoon you have carefully constructed around yourself. Love and fear cannot peacefully co-exist. You must let go of one to grab hold of the other.

Choose love.

Do you have promises from God you are waiting on? Is fear stopping your forward movement? Are you asking Him to equip you before you make a move?

You may want to look behind you.

Your wings may already be there.

It is time to fly.

The following stories are my personal love notes and conversations with God as He nudged me to outgrow my safe and confining cocoon. Some of the encounters will overlap and seem repetitious as you follow my journey. As I said earlier, He had to repeat Himself often to make sure I believed without a doubt in His big love for me. You may take some convincing too. In the meantime, this little prayer may help get your journey started.

Oh Father, thank you for loving me today, in this moment. Your face is looking into mine and Your eyes are deep pools of pure love. You are not waiting for me to get it right. You are not impatient with my slow progress. Thank you for loving me in this moment with complete acceptance and joy.

And thank you for the glorious wings I carry and that will carry me. Amen

two

DROP THE BUCKET

THE ATMOSPHERE AROUND ME was too quiet and sleepy. That's fine when you are at home, on your couch at the end of the day. But this was a cold and stormy morning during our ministry school worship time where I was on staff. We were trying to connect with God with the help of a CD rather than the usual live band that day. I watched the wind outside our classroom windows push the huge trees around as if they were nothing, and it reminded me of the Bible passage we were all studying that week.

Psalm 29 included these words…

> *Give unto the Lord, O mighty ones; give unto the Lord glory and strength. Give unto the Lord the glory due His name;*

> *worship the Lord in the beauty of holiness.*
>
> *The voice of the Lord is over the waters; The God of glory thunders; The Lord is over many waters. The voice of the Lord is POWERFUL; The voice of the Lord is full of MAJESTY.*
> Psalm 29:1-4 NKJV

I read it aloud to the class while the winds were whipping the trees around outside our windows. Everyone responded with happy praises and exclamations of God's might and goodness and worthiness, telling Him how wonderful He is. As I continued to praise Him on my own, I became overwhelmed with God's amazing power and size in comparison to little old me.

My thoughts began to tumble over one another with awe.

> *He is SO vast,*
>
> *SO limitless,*
>
> *SO completely immeasurable!*

As I contemplated the vastness of God, another surprising thought entered my mind.

> *His LOVE for me is just as big and limitless as WHO HE IS!*

Can I repeat that? His LOVE for me is just as big and limitless as WHO HE IS!

He just kept telling me that His love for me was huge and unending. He loved me so much, that in His eyes I could do no wrong. Nothing I do, could appear bad or wrong in His all-loving eyes.

I could do no wrong.

Like a brand new parent whose newborn can do no wrong. A new parent thinks every "coo" and facial expression is adorable and entertaining. But even a mother's love may alter and diminish. It can become faulty and cruel. This is where God's love differs from that of a human parent. His love is perfect. His love is without fear and without boundaries or ending.

God loved me like that and much more, and He wanted me to know it that morning. As the waves and waves of His love began to come over me, I actually felt afraid and I heard myself praying. *"It's too much God, it's too much!"*

I thought I could not contain it anymore. And I was right. The dictionary definition of "contain" is: *"Restrain, to keep under proper control."*

Then I saw an inward picture of myself on a beach with a bucket in my hands. I was trying to catch His love. Like trying to catch the ocean waves. He wanted me to drop the silly bucket and let the waves of love overwhelm me and carry me away.

This all took place within minutes, while I knelt in the back of a classroom full of students. Getting "carried away" was NOT my favorite thing. I like to be in control. In fact, I had been giving myself credit for imagining a bucket rather than a little cup. I grew up singing a song in church with the chorus of "Fill my cup Lord. I lift it up Lord. Come and fill this thirsting of my soul." So I thought I was being pretty brave to discard the little cup and hold up a bucket instead.

But God's love was way too much for my bucket, way too much to contain and control and use. It was more powerful than my ability to stand up to it. Before long, I was lying on the floor. What else could I do? My God's love for me was quite literally OVERWHELMING!

God's love for you is as big as He is!

Are you trying to contain God's love? Trying to keep it in order and control? The old hymn about holding our "cup" up to him to fill and quench our thirsting soul was a small and completely inadequate measure for what He wants to give us.

On that stormy morning in our ministry school, I felt I was being very generous and thinking big, to hold up a bucket instead of a measly little cup. But God was not, and is not, satisfied with either of those containers. No container will suffice. His delight is to knock us off our feet with His powerful waves of love. Tumble us over and over until we are gasping for air and laughing with the freedom of it all!

It can be frightening to be out of control. For some of us it is our greatest fear. But to be out of control WITHIN His control is true freedom and delight. To try to understand it, analyze it or contain it is impossible. God was showing me that it was time to stop trying. Is He showing you this today?

Give up.

It is time to drop our buckets and allow the waves of God's love to sweep us off our feet!

YOUR TURN

Dear Friend, it is time to drop your bucket. It is time to forget about sticking your big toe in the water to test out the temperature and depth. The love of God for you is as huge as WHO He is. His love for you is bigger than the weather; it is stronger than the storm you may be enduring.

Let go of control. Have you ever tried to control an ocean wave? I remember getting tossed about in the ocean waves of Hawaii. I could not get the "jumping into the waves" timing just right. There is a trick to it. Every time I jumped, the wave grabbed me and turned me upside down and over and under until I did not know which way was up. It was scary and totally disorienting. More than once, I ended up with my face in the sand, looking nowhere near as cool as the beauties in the beach movies manage to look. Looking cool and in control is not an option.

The Father's love for you is as relentless and unending as the crashing waves of an ocean. They do not stop, do not give up and do not dry up.

Drop your bucket, feel the sand loosen under your feet and allow the wave to hit your knees and take you with it.

Surrender. It is love.

> *Thank you God, for loving me with relentless love. I let down my guard and say, "yes" to your love. It is scary to me, but I*

surrender to you. I trust You and the love that overwhelms. You are good. You are kind, and You love me with all the power that I see in earthly storms and mighty ocean waves. Sweep me away! Amen three

ERASE SUSIE

IT IS MY TYPICAL SATURDAY morning. Envision the "glamorous life" of a pastor's wife in a small church. I am scrubbing hard at the painted brick walls of our tiny church nursery. The glossy white paint is looking better once the crayon marks are wiped away. I'm glad to be done with my least favorite part of the nursery cleaning; navigating our bulky vacuum cleaner around the spidery legs of two baby swings, a changing table and the grungy-looking playpen.

The plastic blocks have been retrieved from behind the playpen. *Why was some little toddler diligently tossing them back there every single Sunday? Must be a favorite game.*

The stinky plastic diaper pale has been emptied, scrubbed and is sitting out in the sunshine with the hope that nature will be able to remove the aroma that I could not.

God and I were having a conversation as I removed the creative artwork from the wall. The topic was my favorite subject: me. Actually, I should say that it was a somewhat one-sided conversation. God was not saying much.

At first.

I told Him how much I wanted to be like Him. I told Him that I was hungry to help the people in our small, closely-knit congregation. I felt desperately lacking in the ability to do what needed to be done. I had little talent and even less strength in the area of people skills. My prayer was that God would use me in spite of my very obvious defects in personality and leadership experience.

At one point, my exact words were, *"Please get Susie out of the way so that You can shine through."* It seemed like a perfectly reasonable and even noble request.

But God did not let my request go unanswered for long. I immediately heard Him say, *"No! I will NOT erase Susie. I made her and will use who she is!"*

I had fallen into the trap of comparing myself to others whom I admired. I saw how easily and smoothly they led committees and large groups. I watched and listened to them give sound advice and it seemed as if wisdom simply poured out with little preparation or stress. I was convinced that God was burdened with an extra-complicated person in me. Maybe He was waiting for me to get out of the way and stop making His job so hard.

I do not know who coined this phrase but it has been widely shared; "Be you, everyone else is taken." Why do we assume God wants to change us into something completely different when we come to

Him?

He designed us.

He chose our quirks, weaknesses and strengths.

God knows us.

We were made on purpose... not by accident or happenstance. My personality is not an accident. The fact that I over-think before I speak is not a random deformity in my character. It is not something to overcome. God has no desire to erase my foibles in order to give me a makeover. He is not interested in an army of Stepford Christians.

He is a God who loves variety.

In the following weeks and months after this short conversation with God, I was to discover that my quiet demeanor was not a fault or a detriment to God's purposes. God refused to delete me in order to use me. My lack of colorful flamboyance made me a safe and comforting person to certain people in need. My self-analyzing reserve helped people trust me. Steadiness is important in the healing process and I could do that. I could be steady. I could be calm and stable for the people around me who were hurting and confused.

God knows us.

He knows you.

Perhaps you've never suffered from being too quiet. Maybe you have been accused of being too loud. You've had people tell you to take it down a notch and stop being so bossy or bold. Do you find yourself regretting the words that have spilled from your mouth in a moment of passion? You might have a long list of events when you've had to go back and apologize for your forthrightness. Apologies are called for if you have injured someone with your words, but do not berate the way you were created. Do not disparage the way God designed you. Again I say to you that God does not make mistakes. You are not an "Oops!" creation. He likes variety.

God needs people who will speak up. Most great movements in history began with an outspoken person... someone who did not over-analyze their words before letting them loose.

You may hate the crazy cowlick in the back of your hair. He does not. You may have been trying to speak up more, or covering your mouth after saying too much. God designed you carefully, my friend. He was not being absent minded on the day you were created. You have a distinct reason for being alive and He gave you the tools you need to be exactly what He wanted.

He loves you today, just as you are.

He delights in you even when you do not.

He loves you even when you do not.

YOUR TURN

What will this self-acceptance look like for you?

The next time you are in a group of people, be aware of how you interact with them.

- Are you trying too hard to be the funny one when you'd rather be the listener?
- Are you worrying too much about how your addition to the conversation may not be worthwhile?
- Do you find yourself nodding in agreement to an opinion, when deep inside you really disagree?

The answers to these questions will reveal your self-acceptance level. It may be time to practice being the real you, whether the quiet one or the loud one, it is time to be the one designed by God. Be the one He had in mind while your limbs and heart were being formed before your day of birth.

Father, thank you for creating me as I am. You know that I am not crazy about some parts of who I am. Can I ask You today to help me see what You see when you look at me? Could You give me a clue about why You designed me the way You have? Thanks God, I am listening and watching for Your answer in the coming days. I love You and trust You. Amen

four

THAT TIME GOD DID A VAL KILMER IMPRESSION FOR ME

I SIT QUIETLY, STARING at the backs of my eyelids, waiting. I can see nothing but blackness. What else would you expect from behind closed eyes? I am dreading the sharing time that is about to happen because I have nothing to report. The room is quiet and I am fidgeting in my chair.

The guest speaker at our ministry school has instructed us to close our eyes and quietly ask God this question; *"Who do You want to be for me at this time in my life?"* This was not a new or unusual activity for our small school. We know that God is always communicating with us, and that we just need to stop and listen in order to hear Him. Or, in this case, to "see" Him.

But on this day I was in no mood for it. I could easily imagine that the others in the room would dreamily report visions of walking in flowering fields with God. They will describe pictures of being nestled in His comforting arms. I saw blankness and blackness behind my eyelids, and I seriously considered leaving the classroom to go to the bathroom for a few minutes so that I wouldn't have to feel embarrassed by my lack of vision-ability. I am one of the leaders of the school, after all.

With a deep sigh, I ask God to show me Himself and I wait again. My eyes suddenly pop open. I look around.

Did I really hear what I think I just heard?

Yes, it was real, but it was not from anyone around me. I distinctly and clearly heard Val Kilmer say to me,

"You're my chuckleberry."

Did God just do a Val Kilmer impression for me?

I love the movie "Tombstone" where Val Kilmer, playing Doc Holiday, has a habit of muttering, *"I'm your huckleberry."* I had not seen the movie in years, so it was not on my mind. I was waiting for God to show me something about Himself and He chose to show me His funny side, and at the same time tell me that I give Him pleasure.

I am His chuckleberry... whatever that means. I don't care. As I write about this experience some years later, it occurs to me that He really wasn't answering the question posed to Him.

God has a funny tendency to answer a question in a way that forces us to rethink our question. *"You're my chuckleberry."* He told me who I was for Him even though I had asked who He wanted to be for ME. Sitting here in my study, listening to gentle music and my dog snoring on the chair next to me, I am overwhelmed once again at the personal God that I serve and love.

> *I give Him pleasure? I make Him smile and chuckle? How can this be?*

The idea that the great Creator of The Universe can experience enjoyment and pleasure from His relationship with me makes me feel very small… and extremely huge.

> *He will yet fill your mouth with laughing and your lips with rejoicing.* Job 8:21 NKJV

> *A merry heart does good like a medicine, but a broken spirit dries up the bones.* Proverbs 17:22 NKJV

I sometimes wonder if God gets a little bored with our stuffy, contemplative, quiet times with Him. Maybe He just wants to have fun with us on some days. Somewhere along the line we have accepted the false idea that all He wants to do is sit up there in a big chair and judge us.

Think about it. This is the Creator who imagined elephants, giraffes and the hippopotamus! He must have a sense of humor and delight about the world He assembled for us. Didn't God put the need for levity and laughter into our personalities in the first place? He is the original inventor of laughter and giggles, right?

If I am providing Him with a few chuckles every now and then, that's fine by me.

YOUR TURN

Is your spirit crushed? Does joy feel like a distant dream? It could be time to try a little experiment. Tomorrow morning, begin your day with this goal in mind: To find the humor in one thing. A clear symptom of depression is when it feels like every part of your life is a mess. It is usually not true, but it feels true. And that's enough to cause you to sink deeper and lose hope.

> *A crushed spirit dries up the bones.* Proverbs 17:22 NKJV

Today is the perfect day to refuse to sink deeper. This is the day. Tell God how you feel in this moment. Yes, He already knows your heart, but He loves to hear your voice. Tell Him that you are ready for a new view, a new perspective. Sometimes we must determine to look in an entirely new direction in order to change our view. To change our hearts.

Today is the day.

Water your spirit with this prayer:

> *Father God, I feel alone and empty. Hopelessness has weighed me down and I can see no escape from the crush of it. I need You, Father. I cannot talk myself out of this place.*
>
> *Today I have been challenged to be brave and to ask You to show me something funny in this day. My heart is thirsty for water and a fresh taste of joy. Only You can do this. Please*

reveal a bit of Your humor to me today. Thank You. I promise to be listening and watching for You. Amen.

five

DANCE WITH ME

HAVE YOU EVER SEEN a picture with your heart, rather than your eyes? It is one of those ethereal experiences that include all of your senses. Aroma, texture, temperature and mood are almost more real than reality. The moment is more filled with substance than the floor beneath your feet or the people all around you.

I was enjoying a sweet time of worship with my friends on a typical Sunday morning. We were gathered around the front platform of our church sanctuary and the band was playing a favorite song that included the words,

> *"Dance with me, oh Lover of my soul…"*

I close my eyes and gently sway with the beautiful live music. The scene in my mind began with me dancing with Jesus. It is one of my favorite scenes to imagine during my times of worshiping Him. I love to "go there", and this time it was delightful as we moved together with the soft music in the sanctuary.

But without warning the scene suddenly changes without me deciding to change it. I saw, felt, sensed and heard God The Father step up and tap Jesus on the shoulder and whisper,

"She's mine."

Now don't write me off just yet. This may be hard to believe, I know. Please stay with me, because it gets so beautiful.

God took me in His great arms and leaned over me with a size I am struggling to describe for you. I felt so small, but so precious and cherished. I hope it does not mess up the picture, it will not do it justice, but the feeling and size reminded me of watching Beauty and the Beast in the animated movie when they had their glorious ballroom dance. He was so enthralled with Beauty and he leaned over her with such care and gentleness.

But in my heart-picture, even more impacting than His great bulk, were His eyes. The eyes of my Father God were liquid with mighty love for me. He simply could not take His eyes off of me. I was His protected prize. He was drinking me in and delighting in dancing with me!

I was totally comfortable with Him as we glided all over the ballroom of my heart. A daughter who is adored by her father has a grace and confidence that cannot be faked or learned. My Father God's dance with me instilled a new sense of who I am. It was as if He was building up my inner strength and confidence as we swirled the room together. I am His daughter... His beloved daughter. He loves me completely and is proud to be dancing with me in His arms.

I cannot adequately describe this deep experience to you here with these inadequate words. When I got home that day I spent nearly an hour searching online for a picture of ballroom dancers that carried what I felt. No drawing or photo caught what I saw and experienced. But isn't that the wonderful beauty of our own individual relationships with God? What I saw is all mine. What you see, feel and hear when alone or even in a crowd with God, is all yours.

A.W. Tozer said,

> *"An infinite God can give all of Himself to each of His children. He does not distribute Himself so each may have a part, but to each one He gives all of himself as fully as if there were no other." God's Pursuit of Man,*
>
> A.W.Tozer, Moody Publishers

I am God's beloved daughter. You are God's beloved child.

YOUR TURN

Can you take some time to close your eyes and dance with Him as His dearly beloved child?

His arms encircle you completely.

God has surrounded you with Himself.

He is your mighty protector and gentle benefactor. You sway together in a sweet slow dance that makes you feel safe and more secure than at any other moment in your life.

Let Him hold you and convince you of His love.

It is real.

You may be imagining the dance, but you are not imagining His love for you. It is real. It is more real than the room you are in right now.

> *Dear Father, Thank you for our dance. The memory still brings me a smile and a sigh of pleasure. I ask You today to share our dance with those who want to be held by You.*
>
> *Allow this dear reader to rest back into Your powerful arms and know they are safe, safer than they have ever been.*
>
> *Thank You God. Thank You for the dance. Amen.*

six

HE LOVES ME, HE LOVES ME NOT

WE'VE ALL DONE IT. Even if the actual words did not pass our lips while pulling petals from a daisy, we uttered them silently. *"He loves me, he loves me not."* Well, I'll admit it, even if you won't.

I was boy-crazy from even before junior high. Then it got serious. Does that cute brown haired boy in seventh grade science class like me or not? Did the tall blond guy in my youth group just look at me or was that my imagination? EYE CONTACT!! True love!! Before you know it that special someone's name is all over my Pee-Chee folders, surrounded by little red hearts and exclamation points.

Did you ever use the apple stem system to figure out whom you would marry someday? We would slowly twist the apple stem while saying a letter of the alphabet with each turn of the stem. The letter spoken as the stem finally broke off would be the first letter of your future husband's name! I will confess that I twisted harder or softer according to my latest crush. Another trick I used was choosing either the first or last name according to how weak the stem was becoming under my fingers.

As a grown-up, I employed the daisy petal method to see if God loved me. While I no longer used a literal daisy to find out how God felt about me, my inner belief regarding His fickle thoughts about me were very similar to the old flower-killing system. Yesterday God may have loved me, but today I totally blew it with my kids, so He is probably hanging His head in disappointment now.

My sleep ritual was to look over my day and decide if it had been a day worthy of God's love or not. If I had failed him, I would ask His forgiveness and determine to do better the next day. Can you imagine how many nights I went to sleep with a heavy heart? I could so easily picture my God's great face full of sadness over my behavior. *"He loves me not."*

One day may be full of victory and "points" because I had ministered to someone or was extra patient with my boys. Maybe I led a women's Bible study and got up early to spend time in prayer. As a pastor's wife I had plenty of ways to add to my scoreboard every day, right? But sadly, even the full-on ministry days were often riddled with "failures". I could always find the spot in the day where I did not measure up to the high standards of a "Godly woman" in my eyes.

Going to sleep with a heart determined to do better the next day may sound like a noble and even honorable way to better oneself. But I do not believe it is honoring to God. He is not measuring His children each night to see how they have grown, or not grown. His love is not on a sliding scale. Moving up and down according to our actions, obedience and faith.

God does not love me more on my "good" days than my "bad" days. He simply loves me. I do not disappoint Him when I mess up. He does not hang his head in despair when I make the same mistake 20 times in a row. Even as I write that, it is difficult to believe!

Why is it so hard to believe God loves you and me every single day no matter what we do? Because it is not the way we love. We want to love others well. We say we love them unconditionally. But our love is limited. Our love can change and grow or diminish. God loves in a completely different way than we do.

His love is constant.

His love is true and pure.

God's capacity to love is immeasurable and limitless.

We cannot outrun it or escape it. God is delighted with His children... all of us. He sees the good, the bad and the ugly, and still He loves with abandon. Our actions simply do not affect His love toward us. If God could love us more on some days than on others, it would mean His love is conditional and less than perfect. Are you willing to make that accusation of Him? Of course not.

YOUR TURN

You know that God IS love. But you may wonder what this looks like in your daily life. Your life may be complicated and painful in this season.

So you look around and ask, *"Where is Your love, God? I really can't see it today."* And this is a fair question, a question that will lead to the answer, if it is asked honestly. I believe He will show you where His love is if you ask Him. You do not have to shout the question because He is close to you and ready to show you where His love is in the middle of your awful situation.

Ask Him.

God, the Father, the Gentle, the Mighty, the Holy Creator of The Universe loves you! He designed all of the daisies and apples in the world to spell out His name as your one true love. The next time you pull petals or twist an apple stem, I hope you will be whispering these words: *"He loves me, He loves me, He loves me, He loves me. . . ."*

> *Dear God, I know that You love me. But I am struggling to SEE it in the middle of this circumstance. Where are You for me in this situation? I sometimes feel like I am on my own. Can You please open my eyes to see You here today? Thank You, I will be watching and listening for You. I thank You in advance for the love message that I will receive soon. Amen.*

seven

PRACTICALLY A ONE-SIDED LOVE AFFAIR

I QUIETLY WALK INTO the prayer gathering feeling dry and empty. I am glad to be a little bit late because conversation with people is the last thing I want right now. I have nothing to offer God and I am convinced that He must be at least a tiny bit disappointed in me. But it is a prayer gathering so I do what I know how to do. Closing my eyes, I begin to say words of worship I do not really feel. Sometimes this is the right thing to do and it has brought me into God's presence. But this time God interrupts me with these words:

"I don't need anything from you at all."

What did He just say?

I sit there and try to believe those words.

Excuse me? What?

Don't you need my worship?

"No."

Don't you need my sacrifice?

"No."

Don't you need me to love you back?

"No."

His love for me is not based on what I can give Him.

I picture a little toddler girl who loves a soft rag doll. The toddler's eyes light up every time she sees the doll, and she grabs it up and loves on it. The doll does absolutely nothing to deserve such huge love. It doesn't even love the girl back; it is just there.

Can you believe that God loves you like that? Are you trying to earn His love?

Let me tell you that He already loves you. He would gladly trade all of your hours of working for Him into quality time just being with Him. Your hours of preparing the women's Bible study or the years you have spent on the mission field do not add to His love for you. For some believers, this truth will be a bitter pill to swallow. God's love for you is a fact, a permanent reality. He is not dependant upon reciprocation.

For Him it is almost like being involved in a one-sided love affair. When I stop and consider how much God loves me, and I realize that my love for Him is so tiny and full of conditions; it feels like He is definitely not going to receive as much as He is giving. The amazing part is that He is not even surprised or upset about the unequal relationship we have. If God is surprised or upset about anything, it would be why His kids have such a difficult time believing His love is total and requires nothing from us.

When God thinks of you, He smiles. He loves you just because you breathe. When you woke up this morning and threw your legs over the side of the bed, He already loved you. If God carried a wallet or a smart phone, your photo would be in it, and He would bring it out often to show you off. Those are silly ideas that you have heard before, but do they help you grasp the reality of His love?

Some may say this belief will lead to lazy and entitled Christians. But when God spoke to me about not needing anything from me, it did not cause me to walk away from that prayer time with an attitude of cockiness or inflated pride. In fact, the complete opposite occurred within me. His words melted me into tears of gratefulness and a desire to give Him more of myself. God's huge love is a very humbling thing to accept. But it is all He is asking us to do. Just accept His love. Accept it in all of its completeness and joy. It is time for us to learn to enjoy this amazing love affair!

YOUR TURN

Why are you doing what you do? Working for God and to further His kingdom is not wrong, it is certainly not a waste of your time and energy. But it is important to look at your motivation for what you are doing. Examine your reasons for the church jobs you are giving yourself to. Look at your calendar that is crowded with community service and club committees. Too many volunteers have not honestly volunteered. They have been bullied or manipulated into doing what others think they should be doing. Do not allow others to "should" on you. The church martyr syndrome is alive and well, sadly. But it is futile and a waste of time if the goal is to earn more of God's love. You cannot gain more of something you already own completely.

Dear friend, maybe just now, as you finish this chapter, it is the perfect moment to take this in and believe the words you have read.

Take a deep breath.

Let yourself relax into your chair.

You are loved.

Right now in this instant, you are loved and adored by God.

There is no "To Do" list in His hand. He is thrilled with who you are today and tomorrow and yesterday. He is not a needy God. He is not waiting for you to get it right. He is enthralled with the "you" that you are in this moment.

Thank you Father, for not asking me to earn Your love. Thank you for loving me even before my feet hit the floor today.

In this moment right now, I hold up to You, the only gift I have in my hands. I give You myself. It is all I have to offer.

Thank you for sighing in pure delight at the gift I hold up for You. For whispering, "It's all I ever wanted." Amen

eight

DIRTY GOBLET

"LOOK AWAY... I AM HIDEOUS!" Those five words describe my attitude and my prayer life for many years as I longed to make myself into someone worthy of God's love. I had stacks of binders and notebooks from Christian women's retreats and conferences where I scribbled down all the "How-To" rules and formulas that would please God. The ladies up there on the platform in their brightly colored, tailored jackets always seemed to have it all together so perfectly... perfect enough to be experts on the subject.

Shortly after one of those conferences I was at home in groveling-prayer mode. I felt guilty about not giving God enough of my day to be alone with Him.

I was bent over with remorse before God because I was convinced He must be very disappointed in me.

> *How could He still love me and be pleased when I had not had a special "quiet time" with Him in days and days?*

Here is the tricky part of this seemingly simple problem; my overwhelming guilt about not coming to God was keeping me from facing Him. I could not even apologize to Him because I felt I did not "deserve" forgiveness.

Not coming to God was preventing me from coming to God. It sounds silly now, but I believe it is a popular trick of the enemy. He successfully uses us against us. We ask ourselves if we deserve a second, third and fourth chance with God and of course the answer is a resounding, *"No!"*

So there I sat in my favorite chair with a journal and pen in hand, listing my horribleness to God. I tell Him that I do not deserve to come to Him. My hand is beginning to write more about being depressed and unworthy when I hear a small word in my heart and mind. It was simply, ***"Come."***

That is all.

My head spins.

> *Are you sure Father? I am in the middle of my mess. How can you not care about my garbage, my complaining and neglect of you? You want me to list my sins out for you right? How else can one repent? I really need to repent of...*

His only answer is the one word, *"Come."*

In my imagination I saw a picture of a large goblet. It was encrusted with powdery dirt. I could not even see what metal it was made of because it was so covered in dry dirt. But God was using the cup. He handled it as if it was a true treasure, taking great care as He used it for Himself and for others.

I saw that the more He used the dirty cup, the more layers of dirt came off and the gold began to show through. God's hands around the cup were automatically cleaning it while He used it and making it into something glorious. I knew the cup represented me. He was cleaning it gently at the same time as He helped me minister to others: my family, my church, and my friends.

My lesson in God's unconditional love is a recurring theme in my life. It seems that I need to hear and see the truth again and again. This deep inner question of His love for me has led me to fill binders, journals and spiral notebooks with copious notes from sermons and teachings about the love of God.

It still really feels like we should earn it. But that is the view of an earthly human who simply cannot fathom the reality of God-size love. God's love for His children cannot be compared to our love for one another. We try and the Bible even tried…

> *Can a woman forget her nursing child, and not have compassion on the son of her womb? Surely they may forget, yet I will not forget you. See I have inscribed you on the palms of my hands.* Isaiah 49:15, 16 NKJV

> *When my father and my mother forsake me, then the Lord will take care of me.* Psalm 27:10 NKJV

Our person-to-person love is the only template we have, so it is normal to use it as a measuring stick or standard. But it does not work when measuring God's love.

The little picture that God showed me of the dirty goblet illustrates a few different truths.

#1 God is not waiting for me to clean myself up before He loves me and treats me tenderly.

#2 God will still use me before I am clean. By "use me" I mean that He can still speak through me to others and guide me into situations where I can point people to Him.

This is a big deal! I am a dirty, dusty vessel and the Ruler of The Universe loves me completely, as is! Sitting in my comfy living room chair with pen and journal in hand, all ready to list my sins and He stopped me and sent my head spinning and swirling with the truth of His big-love. I emptied my hands, leaned my head back and smiled up at Him. A deep breath escaped me and my eyes overflowed with tears of thankfulness.

I am loved.

YOUR TURN

My Friend, God the Father loves you unconditionally and without reserve. All of His thoughts for you (and there are many) are good. He never looks at you and sighs with impatience at your constant failures or mistakes.

He just doesn't.

God the Father does not love the future you, the new and improved you. His adoration of you is not based on your possible high potential. It is easy to think that God looks at you with high hopes for the great person you could become if you'd just try a little harder. No, He is enjoying the YOU that you are today. Right this minute and the next and the next.

Breathe that in.

Say it aloud to yourself. *"God loves me today, right now, this minute."*

Now try it again without rolling your eyes and shaking your head "no" while you say the words.

> *Thank you Father for loving me today. It is hard for me to grasp this kind of love. It really is! I am opening my heart and my mind to You today so that You will drop this truth into me. I know it will be an ongoing battle to believe that You love me so unconditionally. But I am ready for that battle and together we will win. Thank You, My God. Amen*

nine

DON'T SHOULD ON ME

I WAS RAISED IN THE church, my family attended services twice on Sundays, every Wednesday night and any other time that stuff was happening. Our church was like a wonderful extended family and I loved the way it became a warm and comfortable social circle for me.

The center of that circle was the shared desire to serve God in all areas of our lives. We were taught to read our Bibles everyday, attend church as much as possible and spend time in prayer everyday. As a teen I can remember starting one Bible-reading system after another, marking my calendar with my self-assigned Bible passage to read each day. I would open my highlighted pink Bible and some days it seemed alive as the words on the page fit exactly what I needed that day.

But I also had many days when the words meant nothing to me and made no sense or were just so boring I had to literally force myself to finish so I could make the little check mark on my calendar. This manner of "serving God" came with me into my adult life.

Though this training was well intentioned, it planted the idea that I needed to earn my way into God's heart. If I missed a day of reading or praying, I felt guilty and was constantly feeling that I did not, and could not, measure up as a real Christian.

I remember lessons that compared our spiritual relationship with God to our earthly relationship with boyfriends and girlfriends. One illustration had to do with Bible reading and spending time in devotional prayer. We were asked why we can't wait to spend time with or read letters from our earthly boyfriend or girlfriend, yet we put off spending time with God. The inference was, if we really, truly loved God, it would be easy and natural to read our Bibles and spend time in prayer everyday. This thought brings heaviness to me even now as I write this.

Haven't we all heard Christians around us talking about how they don't read the Bible enough? How often do we hear believers complain about not spending enough time in prayer? But what would you call an earthly love relationship if the partner created a chart to keep track of all the days you missed spending time with him and held it against you? What if you walked around with guilt and fear due to your lack of reading his letters or calling him on the phone often enough? Wouldn't you call that an abusive relationship?

Playing golf on Sunday, going fishing or staying home to watch the game on TV were all evidence of falling away from God or "backsliding". Can't you just picture God up there checking the Sunday morning roll sheet? I am intentionally not mentioning the specific denomination because I believe this mindset of earning God's love is seen in a general way in almost all types of organized religion.

For the last several years God has been showing me a brand new way of looking at Him and the relationship between the two of us. For me the "Good News" is not just about Jesus dying on the cross for my sins. The Good News is that when He said, "It is finished," it was FINISHED! (John 19:30) Any kind of striving or working to dutifully "serve" God because I owe it to Him is not a love relationship. Striving and working fall under the "should" category and God does not "should" on me.

To make myself read the Bible everyday in order to gain points with Him is silly because He has already awarded me all the points available. All of the points. *It is finished!* I don't need to grovel or do penance for my mess-ups. I am forgiven. What I do now is get up, brush myself off and bask in how much He already loves me. This new picture of God is more fun and freeing in everything I do. He loves creativity and adventure and exploration and variety. Can you imagine how a God like that must get pretty bored in some of our church services? Do you ever get bored there?

Be honest now.

The God-relationship I enjoy today includes us doing chores together, driving together and watching movies in one another's company. Hey, my God even did a Val Kilmer impression for me once! What would you do if you heard that and you knew it was God? Yah, that's what I did... I laughed out loud and couldn't wait to tell the others what I had heard!

This is not the same God who "shoulds" on people! Whenever I hear myself saying the "should" word to others or to myself, it becomes highlighted like the spell-check on my laptop. I stop and re-examine what I am saying or thinking.

> *Am I agreeing to be on that committee because I want to or because I should?*

God may not be impressed with or even affected by my service to Him when it is done dutifully because "someone" had to do it. I have been surprised at how the world did not come to a sudden halt when I "failed" to do what I "should".

What freedom this brings!

I believe the church leaders of the past had good intentions. They insisted we do our Christian disciplines because that is how they were trained and how they lived. But it is also why so many Christians in the past looked and sounded burnt out and angry when they preached. That is not the life I live. Mine is joyful, surprised and full of pleasure and delight most of the time. The God I love is full of goodness and kindness. I could tell many stories about both giving and receiving "shoulds" after being in vocational ministry for many years. But I will end with this: **Should happens, but not to me if I can help it!**

YOUR TURN

You and I now live in a culture that glorifies the problem of being too busy. Social media articles, status updates and real life friends who gather together, seem to spend a great deal of time complaining about their overly busy lives. In reality they are bragging about being too busy, as if it is a good thing.

As if it is evidence of the good life and success.

The truth is, an over-packed life is not a healthy life. A crammed-full calendar could actually be symptomatic of allowing others to "should" on you. It might be time to list your activities and get ruthless about eliminating the items that do not give you joy or fulfillment. Ask yourself why you agreed to lead the women's Bible study or Kids' Church once a month. Yes, they needed the help, but it is important for you to ration your energy and passion in the best way possible for you and your family.

In any normal church or community organization there are a few people who do everything and a lot of people who do very little. It is time to spread the opportunities out for others to pick up. There is someone in your group who needs and wants to be contributing more. This is the chance to leave an opening for them to step into. If you have volunteer jobs that have lost the fun, it is time to let them go. Do not allow someone else's "should" to get all over you.

Step away from the "should".

Father, I thank You for the gifts You've given me. I want to use them to the best of my ability and bring glory to You in their use. I do not want to be filling holes that You did not design me to fill.

Forgive me for falling into the temptation to glorify myself by taking jobs that were not meant for me in the first place. Please help me trim down my TO DO list and cross out the items that You did not choose for me. I will trust You in this difficult task. Let me see what You see for me. Thank You, Father. Amen ten

GOD LOVES THE WAY HE MADE YOU

ONE OF THE HIGHLIGHTS of the ministry school that my husband and I led for 10 years was our yearly mission trips. We took teams of students to the Philippine Islands, the Fiji Islands and even China. We spent 14 days ministering in spiritual and practical ways, assisting churches, visiting slums and praying door-to-door or hut-to-hut.

I made the Philippines trip four times. My usual "place" on these trips was as a mom-figure to help the (college age and older) students adjust in a different culture and environment. Even though I am just as freaked out as they are!

One year in particular holds the story I want to share with you today. My journal of that trip records a desperate prayer I sent to God.

> *"Father, please bypass my normal reserve and let me be open and comfortable and as loving to them as You would be in the flesh. Thank You for this amazing opportunity to express You and Your love to these people who are without hope."*

My simple prayer was heard and I still smile when I remember how clearly He answered the desire of my heart.

The parts of the trip agenda that I dreaded the most were the slum visits. These are makeshift shantytowns that are the worst I have ever seen in any other country. The "houses" are propped up boards, signs or corrugated metal for the better homes. There is no running water, electricity or sewage system. Dirty diapers, human waste and sludgy mud run freely between the unstable shelters for families as far as the eye can see.

As our group assembled to board the trucks that would take us outside the main city to this land of forgotten people, we were divided up into smaller groups to visit different slum areas. One group was in need of a Team Leader. I was shocked to hear my voice say, *"I'll do it."*

I had three students and an interpreter with me. We began to walk among the streets or pathways that led into the strange and unreal neighborhood. The smells were the first obstacle to overcome. Next we had to figure out where the actual front "doors" were to these homemade houses. When that failed we just called out a "Hello" and waited to see who emerged.

At the first place a young, pretty mom invited us into the walk-in closet-size home. Her three kids were on a bed in the corner. There were no chairs, just the bed and a fan and a TV connected to a long cord. When asked if we could pray for any needs she had, she told us that her kids were all sick. I had been watching her infant since entering. The baby girl was so still for a six month old! She just lay there and stared into space. No sounds or movement at all.

The mom told us that the baby had stomach trouble. I had no idea what to do other than pray this simple prayer with my hand on her tiny body, *"In the name of Jesus, I speak healing to this little tummy."*

The baby immediately perked up and stared into my eyes, cooed and blew some bubbles! We all laughed and she and her mom laughed with us. Our team did not want to leave this wonderful spot of joy. We just wanted to stare into those huge brown eyes that really seemed to be seeing something delightful in us.

After we tore ourselves away and approached the next home, a smiling woman stepped out and communicated that she wanted us to meet her 87-year-old mother inside. Entering her house involved climbing over several levels of mismatched cinder blocks with exposed re bar and garbage. We could not tell what was considered inside or outside.

These ladies graciously asked us to sit on their ripped and ragged green couch. The wall was decorated with a plaster, painted clock with no hands. A movement on the counter revealed a large rat running from one end to the other. Toothless 87-year-old Lola suffered from bad knees and arthritic shoulders. She showed us how she could not lift her right arm up very high.

I told her that just the day before, I had seen a woman with arthritis in her back and hand get healed and that we would love to pray for her. She responded with a huge smile and said she knew Jesus and was so happy we were there to pray for her.

God totally healed her knees while our hands were on them! She bounced her legs up and down again and again. Then I asked if we could pray for her shoulder and she began to make punching, boxing motions with her arms and said it was healed already! As we left she gave us each a sloppy toothless kiss on our cheeks. It was so sweet and funny!

Do you want to know the most shocking miracle of that day? After going to several more families and seeing God do wonderful things both large and small, we felt some tiny raindrops as we moved along the path. I looked up and asked the interpreter if we could keep going to the rest of the homes. She strongly said no, that we needed to get out of the rain. I was honestly disappointed to quit. But she was right. Within another 10 minutes the rain was hard enough that we could barely see and we ran for cover under a large tin-roofed basketball court area. We had to shout to hear one another!

The miracle? It was that I was disappointed to quit! Me, the background encourager who likes structure, planning and cleanliness! God heard and answered my small prayer with a minor change to my request. He did not really "bypass my reserve" as much as He gently used it to bring His presence into the homes of women who may have been frightened or suspicious of a louder and bolder personality knocking on their doors.

God knows me.

He knows you.

We don't want to ask Him to change us.

We want to ask Him to be Himself IN us.

He created each of us with unique gifts, traits and personalities and He knows how to express His huge love through us to others. All we need to do is say Okay. God loves the way He made each one of us. And could it be possible that He considered our personality types as He chose the best way to express His love to this world? It is not beyond consideration that God knows who is still doubtful of His love and who would be the perfect person to answer that question in the best possible way.

YOUR TURN

The Father designed you for a purpose.

To be loved by Him and to share that love with others.

It really is as simple as that. When we actually believe God loves us, it changes everything. When you know you are loved, you are free to give away that love generously and abundantly. You know there is more where it came from; there is no need to be stingy or protective. Love is generous.

God likes your personality. He thought it up and installed it in you. Don't ask Him to change it for a bigger, louder, quieter or fancier version. He wants to send His love to the world through your style and version. Are you quiet, or are you boisterous? Are you methodical or are you spontaneous? He enjoys that about you. He won't answer the prayer to change the way you've been designed. God has created you with love. Like one of those tags that grandmas add to a hand-knitted sweater or blanket; Made With Love.

You are made with love to share love.

> *Father, I take a deep breath and say thank You for making me the way I am. I have struggled with the way You made me and I may have even grumbled about it to You. But today, at this moment I am ready to embrace the person that You created me to be. I accept my quietness or my boldness. I*

thank You for designing me the way that You have. Mostly I thank You for loving me the way that you do! Amen

eleven

GOD'S SONG FOR ME

The Lord your God in your midst, the Mighty One will save; He will rejoice over you with gladness, He will quiet you with His love, He will rejoice over you with singing. Zephaniah 3:17 NKLV

GOD SINGS OVER US? Have you ever thought about that possibility? My daughter-in-law has written a beautiful multi-verse song she sings over our first grandchild. I heard her sing it to him one night when she did not know I could hear her from a different room. It was beautiful and encouraging and full of valuable declarations about who this new little person was and how important he would be to the world. God is a creator and His people are full of creativity too.

Special songs can soothe us and significantly alter our mood in minutes, can't they? Even the robotic and socially awkward Sheldon Cooper on "The Big Bang Theory" admits to needing the comfort of a song in times of stress or illness. He often asks his friends to sing the song from his childhood . . *Soft Kitty, Warm Kitty.*

As silly as that little song is, it was easier to believe than the whispered song I heard during a desperate time of struggle in my life several years ago. I am not musical, so I cannot translate the tune that accompanied this song, but it is in my head and heart forever. I sometimes find myself humming it and I know that God is singing over me.

> ***"You are loved, you are loved,***
>
> ***I am loving you.***
>
> ***You are loved, you are loved,***
>
> ***I am loving you.***
>
> ***I am loved, I am loved,***
>
> ***He is loving me.***
>
> ***I am loved, I am loved,***
>
> ***He is loving me"***

Sometimes He adds my name to make sure I get His message. God is romancing me; He wants me to be close. He is wooing me and drawing me to Himself. The song says the same thing over and over like waves, because He so desperately desires that I believe the words.

I often picture a beach scene and the constant repetition of the waves coming toward me again and again, reminding me of how God's love for me is completely relentless. He knows about my doubts and He is trying to convince me. Like a fairytale lover beneath a window, God is calling, enticing and promising me His complete love.

When this little song slips into my mind and heart it makes me smile, but the intensity is also a little bit scary. I ask myself if I am enough for Him. I wonder how I can possibly be worthy of this attention. His desire is for my complete surrender to Him. Can I do that? God knows my heart, He knows there are areas that are not all His. But this knowledge does not stop His desire or His deep pleasure in me. He sees, knows and wants more. So He is wooing me to give Him more because He loves all of me. Not just the sweet and pure parts, but all of me.

Everything in me wants to just drop into those eyes that are full of so much love. And it is easier to do than most of us think. All it takes is a small nod of the head and the whisper of a "yes."

And He has us.

We are His.

He is loving you.

YOUR TURN

You are His.

He is calling you to move even closer.

God wants you to know that His love for you is complete and true and pure.

As you read these words, I believe Father God is leaning forward in anticipation of you and your response. He knows you, warts and all, and He desires you still.

God is singing over you. Feel free to borrow my simple little song, but I am convinced He has a special song just for you. Ask Him to sing it over you. Why not? It may feel silly, but whatever tune and words that come to mind just may be from Him. Can't hurt to ask, can it? Go for it.

My little song from God came to me way back in 2007, but it is still as clear as ever while I sit here typing this message for you. My eyes are brimming and my heart is excited to know that you may be hearing your very own God song right now. I pray you will hear it and believe that the Ruler of the Universe, the King above all Kings, is singing over you because He adores you and wants all of you for His own.

Dear God, I ask You to share Your song with this reader. Would You open her ears and eyes to the magnitude of Your love for her? Whisper, shout, sing, write a message that cuts through all the doubt and wondering and makes the message of Your love unmistakable and impossible to ignore. Thank You, Father. Amen

twelve

POWERFUL WORDPLAY WITH GOD

OVER THE YEARS, AS I have spent time talking to God and listening to Him talk to me in a variety of ways, He always seemed to be stuck on one theme again and again. At this point in the book, you clearly know what that repeated message is, right?

> ***"Child, I love you."***

> *Well, of course you love me. You are God, You love everyone. You kind of have to, right?*

But time after time this is the message He sent to me. Visiting guest speakers at my church would pray for me and tell me that God really loves me a lot. These would be complete strangers who I'd never seen before and would never see again. I began to sense what was coming as they prayed for me. The big smile would appear on their face and they would look at me with an extra sparkle in the eye.

> *"Wow, God really loves you a lot! He just wants me to tell you that today!"*

In my Bible reading I was constantly finding passages about His love for me. Even the obscure verses that did not use the word "love" screamed out to me about His great love for me. It seemed as if every book I picked up was telling me the same thing. *God loves you, Susie.* I would hear my friends tell of God giving them huge visions and jobs to do in the world. But not me, to me He continued to just whisper intimate, sweet nothings of love in my ear. (I know that I've said this in earlier chapters…but my bad habit of comparing myself to others was a true source of pain and confusion.)

After years of trying to believe that the Holy God of The Universe actually loves little old me, I finally began to grasp it. I started to claim it and revel in it! Me! God loves me! My walk became a bit taller, my smile to others became more genuine and the confidence of knowing I was loved by God affected every part of my life and personality.

Then He began to tell me what He loved about me! He loves my compassion for others, my wisdom from years of walking with Him. God loves my humor and the way I accept people just as they are. He told me things about myself that I did not see yet, some things I still do not see. His idea of who Susie is, far outshines my picture of Susie.

I was full of worry that I was not doing enough for Him. It is so easy to confuse doing with being. God loves who I am, not what I do. I used to worry about falling into a place of "working in vain." I would recall the Bible story about people getting to the throne of God and holding up their good works and charitable deeds. God would look at them and say, *"I never knew you...."* (Matthew 7: 22-23*)*

> *Would those workers for God be shocked and surprised? Did they spend their whole life giving and volunteering in the church nursery, witnessing door-to-door and then get to heaven and be turned away? What if that happened to me? How will I know?*

But God's love-words to me, about me, revealed that He is not concerned with my good works, charitable giving or sacrificial prayer times. He wants to KNOW me.

Know me... not just know what I am doing, but who I am being. God values His relationship with me over keeping track of my workmanship. Relationship weighs heavier than my activity or ability to produce something for Him.

God loves who I am more than what I do.

Knowing who I am has made me stronger. When the little nagging negative thoughts come and try to pull me down, I am better equipped to stand against them. I am not as easily intimidated by negative thoughts about myself. I hope this does not sound arrogant, but I do not allow those doubts about my worth to linger in my mind. I used to wallow in that negative place for weeks and months. That is why my God had to keep sending me those intimate love notes over and over again. He had to repeat Himself and use books, songs and other people to convince me that I am loved, that I am worth being loved by Him.

When God whispered His love words into my heart, it changed my mind. His love transformed my thoughts and altered my self-evaluation. This intimacy with the God of The Universe can only make a person stronger and more confident.

This spiritual intimacy changed my identity. I found my TRUE identity through accepting the love of God. Embracing my true identity made me invulnerable to the lies of the enemy about my worth.

I know who I am.

I know Who loves me.

This changes everything!

I really love words. Look at this...

I have found my identity in my intimate times with God. I have found my ID in my intimate times with God.

Knowing my ID has protected me from negative ideas that try to intimidate me. Our enemy is all about intimidation. Knowing my true identity turns the battle around and into the opposite direction and I begin to intimidate the enemy. No longer am I on the defensive, I move to the offensive.

My INTIMATE times give me my ID and do not allow doubts or fears to INTIMIDATE me.

What is the difference in those two words?

INTIMATE

INTIM***ID***ATE

ID!!

I love that! Cool huh?

YOUR TURN

Dear Friend, God's view of you is more REAL than yours. God's view of you is more TRUTHFUL than what you see or feel about yourself. Ask Him today what He sees when He looks at you.

You may be surprised at His response.

Write down what comes to your mind when you ask God what He sees. It may seem silly or the complete opposite of your view. Record it anyway. Write it down.

God wants you to walk in your true identity, your true ID. This little activity will be harder than expected. The first things on your list will probably be about things that you do rather than things that you are. That's okay. Cross out the "dos" and turn them into descriptions of who you are. For instance, if you wrote down *"I counsel troubled teens"*, change it to *"I care about teens."* See the difference there?

You will find your true identity through intimacy with God. Time alone, time spent listening and asking questions. It is worth the effort because your identity will arm you to intimidate the enemy when he comes with his lies.

Find your **IDENTITY** through **INTIMACY** and **INTIMIDATE** the enemy.

> *Thank You, Father, for words and the beautiful way that You communicate through this little word game. I ask for*

Your sweet nothings whispered in my ear. I ask You what You see when You look at me. What do You feel when You think of me? Please help me to agree with Your answers to these questions. I want to see what You see and believe what You believe about me. Amen thirteen

IT ALL COMES BACK TO LOVE

I WAS A CHURCH YOUTH group girl. In my case, this means that most of my social life was centered around the other kids who attended my church and were involved in the weekly youth group meetings and outings. You would be right in assuming my youth group enjoyed lots of silly games and goofy theme nights. We encouraged team spirit and loved funny skits. But we also loved scripture and Bible discussions.

My small youth group was made up of the usual variety of people found in any church group. Some of the kids only cared about the games and prizes, and others cared about understanding God and figuring how to be like Jesus in everyday life. Most of us loved both.

My future husband moved to our town while he was a teenager and his family joined our church. His parents forced him to attend the mid-week youth group meetings even though he had no desire at all. He did not know God and he rolled his eyes at our enthusiasm for the Bible and how it could be used in the modern day world.

I was one of the student leaders in our youth group, so this meant that I helped organize and plan the meetings and activities. I can still see his smirk as he sat in the back row watching me. It made me all the more determined to convince this guy that God was real and not as lame as he seemed to think.

Totally without my help, God grabbed this guy's attention one night out in the woods in his junior year. The very next week he appeared at school with a big red Bible and a transformed attitude about God. My future husband read everything he could find about Jesus and devoured old and new books about the Bible. Suddenly he was a Jesus freak!

I was smitten.

But he had "no time for women." He was totally consumed with learning all he could about Jesus. His research led to many heated discussions with older Christians and those who were not older, but had been believers longer than him... like me.

Now he sat in the back of the youth meetings and teased me about my simplistic view of God. My naïve response to his complicated new ideas about God and history and the meaning of life was—

> *"All I know is that God loves me and I love Him!"*

This was usually declared with tears streaming, due to my exasperated embarrassment about not being able to join in his deep theological discussions. I tried hard to keep up, but was lost in the twists and turns and layers of questions about where God came from and why He really created us in the first place.

My only retort always came back to, *"All I know is that I love God and He loves me!"*

I felt silly and more than a little bit stupid up against the deep discussions he and his friends seem to savor so much.

Well, my friends, I did eventually marry this Jesus freak know-it-all, and in recent years, he has brought this phrase of mine back to me in a full circle. After more than 25 years of full-time ministry side-by-side and all of the crazy ups and downs that we have survived together, this man now says that I had it right all along.

He loves to remind me of my tearful retort and how my simple, uncomplicated belief in God's love was the deepest truth of all. Somewhere along the line I lost that simple truth, and God spent the rest of my life re-convincing me of His love. Now there are many "new and improved" thoughts about the church, the Creator and our role as believers. Books, articles, blogs and online discussions abound with new thoughts about the true meaning of life and where God fits into what we do each day.

But it all comes back to love.

Thousands of church denominations exist because of the tiny differences we have found in our experiences with God. If we could simply agree on the truth of His love for us and our love for Him, I think the world would be transformed. Yes, this is Susie being simplistic again. It seems to be what I do. But I no longer feel silly or stupid for my simplistic view.

The world is full of variety. God designed it this way. We are not all the same flavor and I believe our differences are not a problem for

God. I don't think He cares that we have divided ourselves up into thousands of denominations and clubs of thought. As long as we can look outside our specific group and agree with the others that God is love.

God loves me and I love Him.

These are the only important facts. When I believe these truths, it will lead to my ability to love others like God loves others. Because when God loves me and I love Him... and He loves the lady over there across the street, I am going to love her too. It happens like that. Too simple? Maybe it's just me, but it is what I believe.

When I am able to grasp that God loves me, with all my mess-ups and flaws, there is a subtle shift that takes place inside. I begin to see others in a more gracious way. I give more grace to the people around me because I know how much grace I have been given. Actually, I will probably never know how much grace God has given me, it is a close companion to his love for me and that is too much to measure.

YOUR TURN

You may be thinking that you don't love Him enough. Your first thought may be that others do a better job of serving God than you do. Can I tell you the truth again?

When we dwell on the idea that we do not love God enough, or properly, or fervently enough, this leads to a tiny wall being built between our Father and us. It causes us to stand back from Him. This wall makes us avoid Him. God is not stepping back from us. He stays the same. But we separate ourselves from Him because we feel unworthy of His attention and love. This self-imposed separation is all based on a lie. Here is the truth…

God does love you. And you love Him.

God loves you, today, right now, as is. Do not allow yourself to dwell in a lie. This moment would be a good time to simply take a deep breath, look up and accept that big love.

> *Father, You always bring me back to love. It is who You are and what You are. Your love carries more weight than any doctrine or theory about You. I come back to the basic truth of Your love for me. How can I say thank you enough? Amen.*

fourteen

MY THOUGHTS ABOUT HIS THOUGHTS

I STEP OUT OF THE clothing store, shopping bags in one hand, shading my eyes against the bright sunshine with the other. I scan the busy parking lot for our car, because as usual I've forgotten where we parked. The longer I stand there, the more uncomfortable I am. It's not the sun that is making me uncomfortable.

My husband is sitting in our car, out there somewhere in the crowded parking lot, watching me and probably getting a pretty good chuckle out of it. How many times have I done this? I am directionally challenged, even needing some guidance when stepping out of a store inside a mall! I always choose the wrong direction to walk. And now my husband is watching me and I am remembering how much he loves to tease me about my lack of car-placement memory.

Then my eyes lock onto his and sure enough, he is grinning from ear-to-ear. I sigh and make my way to the car, throwing the bags in the backseat. I slide into the front seat, buckle my seatbelt and turn to his broadly smiling face, bracing myself for the teasing and ask, *"What?"*

With a sparkle in his eye he says, *"When I saw you standing there, it took me right back to our high school days when I used to watch you come down the school hallway toward me. You are so beautiful!"*

My heart does flip-flops, and I must quickly correct my thinking about his thinking!

I do this to God too. I keep getting it wrong regarding His thoughts toward me.

> *My thoughts are not your thoughts, nor are your ways My ways, says the Lord.* Isaiah 55:8 NKJV

For some reason I tend to think God is unhappy and displeased when He looks at me. But nothing could be further from the truth. The following is a journal entry from when my two boys were little. I was active in more ministry jobs than anyone should ever say "yes" to. My prayer life was lacking. I was asking God to help my family and to give me ideas for the women's Bible study and things like that. But we were spending no quality time together. So this led to guilt and depression and of course, to the belief that God was sitting out there somewhere frowning at me. I felt angry, sorry, alone and crowded all at the same time. Nothing would console me. No more chocolate, coffee, time alone in a long hot bath, nothing. My journal reads...

> *I have been down this road way too many times and God knows that, so how could I ask for forgiveness? My shame is*

keeping me from Him because I do not deserve Him. I am such a mess. I know He will forgive me and that makes me feel even worse!

Now suddenly in the last few hours I am hearing Him whisper to me, "I love you... just come to Me... please."

Just when I am thinking and feeling that all is hopeless He is calling me to Himself. Why? Has He no pride? I haven't even asked for forgiveness yet. Doesn't He want me to beg and plead? He is offering me mercy before I even ask for it; I do not understand His love for me!

God did not make me ask for forgiveness. I did not need to grovel or pay for my crime of neglecting Him. He was not unhappy with me at all. Right in the middle of my misery and blind wandering, He was holding out His mercy to me, even before I asked for it. God was smiling at me and loving me.

His thoughts are higher, full of more grace and patience than I can muster up for those around me. I was making the mistake of imagining that God thinks like I think. That He gets irritated as easily as I do, that He is drumming His fingers on the table waiting for me to get it right.

I do not offer mercy up as easily as He does. I want justice when my family or I are wronged. I want fair treatment. I want recompense and restitution. These are my ways and these are my thoughts.

I am so thankful that God's thoughts are not my thoughts and that His ways are not my ways! God's ways are infused with such overwhelming love that He cannot see us without love in His eyes. He refuses to keep a tally of our wrongs against Him because His vision is colored with mercy.

How else could He be grinning at us across the crowded parking lot when we've messed up for the millionth time?

YOUR TURN

Dear Friend, He is smiling at you today!

God knows you.

He knows what all you are juggling.

He likes you more than you think He does.

When the craziness of life begins to overwhelm you and the kids are pulling at you for attention 24/7, God is there and He understands. He is not impatient with you and your progress or lack thereof. God is not tapping his foot on a cloud wishing you would hurry up and grow up.

God loves you today. He even adores you today! God is better at love than any parent. We call Him Father, but God loves higher and deeper and truer than an earthly father is able. He has no false ideas about you. He knows you. You are His creation and made by His design. What else could He be doing but smiling at you?

All you need to do is look up and smile back.

> *Thank You, God, for smiling back at me, even when I am not smiling. I am worrying and fussing and stressing. But still You refuse to stress or worry. You smile at me. You open Your big arms to me and invite me into them. Thank You for Your relentless embrace, for Your constant grace and forgiveness. Thank You for being the loving God that You are. Amen.*

fifteen

MY SPA DAY

WE HAD BEEN CHALLENGING the students in our ministry school to arrive ready to fully engage in worship as soon as they entered the school worship room each morning. We told them to be prepared to give, to be ready to contribute to the worship experience. Sitting down and becoming a spectator was frowned upon. Simply coasting along and waiting for others to lead them into worship was the lazy way to begin a day of ministry school.

I loved being one of the first people in the worship room each school day. My normal ritual was to turn on the lights, straighten the chairs and throw away scattered papers and cups from the previous day. While doing these mindless tasks, I would walk around between the chairs talking to God before the musicians and students began to trickle in at 8 o'clock each morning. On this particular morning, I wandered around the edges of the room and asked God what He had in mind for the day. What did He want me to contribute? His answer caught me off guard. It went totally against what we had been encouraging the students to do!

God wanted me to sit down and receive. As I walked slowly past the front row of chairs facing the white board, I knew that I was supposed to have a seat there in the front of the classroom, but I argued with Him a bit first. I do not know why I think I can win an argument with God, but I do it all the time! I kept walking and had my say first.

> *But God, everyone will think I am a slacker if I just sit there. They'll wonder why I am not involved and being fully engaged in the worship time!*

Can you hear the whiney tone?

Surprise, surprise, He did not care what the students might think! He told me clearly to sit down, to receive, and to stop thinking so much. He said to stop thinking about thinking.

So I sat on one of the chairs in the front row. I realized I was sitting on the edge of the seat and this was not good enough. So I scooted all the way back against the chair back. Now I was sitting straight up and staring at the whiteboard in front of me. Not good enough. I knew what I needed to do. I scooted my body forward again and forced myself to lean my head back against the chair and close my eyes.

I could hear people coming into the room, the musicians setting up their instruments and students softly praying. A bit of laughter as people greeted one another on this new day. I took some deep breaths and immediately I "saw" a picture of myself with cucumber slices on my closed eyelids. I have never been to a spa, or had a true spa treatment, but this was lovely. I could feel the cool cucumbers on my eyes and I could smell delicious aromas all around me. Then God whispered to me.

> ***"Susie... no job, no agenda, no plan, no talking or even singing. I am pampering you this morning because I love you so much!"***

I allowed my shoulders to relax and I slumped down into the chair even more. Tears are welling as I write about this special moment because the feeling of love is washing over me once again. On that school morning, there on the front row, I began to giggle as another picture came to me. I could see myself cleaning the spa counters with a sponge and trying to slice more cucumbers for all of the people I could hear waiting to come into the massage room! God had to keep telling me over and over again to lie back down and rest.

I heard a student leading one of my favorite songs and I tried to get up and join the singing, but I could not. I wasn't paralyzed, but my body felt heavy and so relaxed that the effort of getting up was simply beyond me. I could hear students dancing near me and jumping really loudly on the floor. The vibrations from their feet pounding on the floor beside me literally went up through my feet and into my bones all the way to my neck, where my tension often shows itself. It felt wonderful. I was getting a neck massage from God!

I began to ask God if I could possibly live in that blissful place. I did not want to leave. I didn't want to "break the spell" by standing up and living a normal day. Could I just stay in that relaxed and slightly "drunk" state of mind all the time?

But even as I asked Him the question, I knew that my life was full of too many jobs that needed to be covered. I was part of a large church staff, a leader of a ministry school. I still had two kids at home who need me, and an afternoon office administration job. All the important "balls" that I was juggling would surely fall to the ground. Our ministry, the school, our family would all fall apart without my full attention. Guess what my God said?

> ***"So you think that YOU are the one holding it all together?"***

Ouch.

What did I learn from this "spa day" from God? What lesson can I pass on to you as you read this little story? I am reminded once again of the verse about how differently God thinks.

> *My thoughts are not your thoughts, nor are your ways My ways, says the Lord.* Isaiah 55:8 NKJV

We are constantly trying to second-guess the God of The Universe. It is so easy to imagine that God looks at our days the same way we do. We want to look back at each of our allotted 24 hours and feel productive. What did we accomplish in our day? What items can be checked off our To Do list?

This sense of accomplishment helps us feel like our lives are worthwhile. We may not say it out loud, but we often fall into a habit of working to be worthy of God's love. One of my greatest desires is to hear Him say, *"Well done…"* This is your hope also, right? It is totally normal to think that the more we do for God, the more we will deserve that "Well done." I mean the very word "done" is one of the past tense forms of the word "do."

But here is my lesson from my spa day; God loves me more than the jobs I do for Him. God had a To Do list for that day and at the top of the list was "Pamper Susie". I could have ignored His prompting to sit down on that first row of chairs in front of my ministry school students. I believe that I still could have had a great day. But not the best day! I would have missed out on another sweet message of how much He loved me. Oh, another important lesson from my spa day; never frown on those who sit while worshiping. We do not know what could be happening between God and the worshiper.

YOUR TURN

God loves you more than what you are doing for Him. God cares more about you than the number of converts you will bring to Him. He loves you more than the perfect Bible Study outline you are working on. His thoughts about you and your worth have nothing to do with how many missionaries you are supporting or how early you are getting up to have devotions.

Your God wants to lavish you with His love today. He wants to pamper you. As you read these words He asks you to take a deep breath. You will probably need to take a few deep breaths. Your God is asking you to let your shoulders fall. You did not even know how hunched up they were, did you?

Now allow the truth of His love to wash over you.

Ignore every thought that may try to pull you away right now.

You are not reading this book and this chapter accidentally today.

Your freedom is on God's To Do list for this moment.

You are His delight. He is looking at you with shining eyes and a smile that reveals a love that has no limits, no boundaries, no disappointment or false expectations.

Take a moment to bask in His love.

It is DELICIOUS!

Father God, I come to you today and try to simply believe that you love me for me, not for what I am doing for you. Everything in me says the opposite. But your thoughts are not my thoughts. Your thoughts are pure and without any agenda other than love. Right now, in this moment I accept your lavish love. I put away any thoughts of worthlessness. You see only beauty when you look at me. You love me. Thank you Father.

sixteen

PRAISING GOD & THREATENING KIDS

WHEN I WAS A YOUNG mom of two active boys, I learned that my special moments with God were NOT going to happen in church. I can distinctly remember standing in our row in the sanctuary and lifting my hands in worship only to bring one hand down to nudge a boy back onto the seat or to replace a toy that one brother stole from the other. Why, oh why, did I feel that the pastoral family needed to sit near the front of the church?

This was, of course, not terribly conducive to sweet communion with God or adoring praise. Closing my eyes was certainly not going to happen. Praising God and threatening kids do not go well together, even though I did try it for quite a while. But eventually I had to accept that my most meaningful times with God would have to happen at home while the boys were napping or at school. Our sanctuary times became much less stressful when I chose to use them as family time to color, sing and have a small snack and cuddle.

What could have been a tough and uphill struggle, actually taught me a very important lesson I still believe: church is not meant for God encounters... at least, it is not meant to be your MAIN God encounter of the week. Church is not designed to be your only source of communicating with Him. No one should see their hours in a sanctuary one morning a week as the most impacting and life changing exchanges with their Creator.

Our times of gathering together are for celebrating what we have been enjoying and discovering about God all week long. This is how I see church. It is a place to rejoice in how amazing God has been to us in our daily lives on the job, at school or in our homes. If we find ourselves depending on the Sunday service for our strength to get through another week, something is wrong.

Gathering together with others of the same faith creates a wonderful synergy. The corporate anticipation is delightful and inspiring. I am convinced that God loves to see us all together, ready to celebrate Him in a group. It's like a family coming together to retell stories of love and relationship.

God loves church. It is easy to imagine the Father watching His children enter the church building or house church, and He is cheered and uplifted to see His children together. He enters the atmosphere along with His kids and His presence can be felt there. He may rejoice as He watches a certain one hug another one. Holy Spirit sweeps through as the music and worship rise from the crowd.

But, it is the one-on-one, intimate times with The Father that will change your life in an instant. Transformation happens within the secret conversations between you and God. Inner decisions that were ignited in the sanctuary are faced with reality at home. When you are alone, the sanctuary decisions are tested and solidified. At home we are most often our truest selves. Your most intimate times with God happen in your home or car or while running. There is no hiding behind the music, the friends or the pew.

As I have compiled these stories of pivotal love encounters with God, I see that very few of them occurred during a church service.

When my sons were little I had a "devotions basket" with my Bible, pens and journal all in one place so I could grab the quiet moments when they occurred. Now, my living room is my sanctuary. When the weather is nice, my backyard makes the perfect spot for time with my God. And here at home there are no rules about keeping a lid on my coffee cup!

YOUR TURN

You may be feeling dissatisfied with your church. You may have heard yourself mutter that church just isn't giving you what it should. The corporate meetings are leaving you hungry for more.

This is not a bad thing.

It might be a good time to step back and look at the expectations you have for church. We know that we need God. It is easy to ask your church to fill your need for God, but it is also unfair. Only God can fill your need for Him. He designed you this way. God created you with a desire for Him. It is tempting to fill that desire with food, money, activity...or church.

If your church is leaving you hungry for more of God, you've found a good church. You can find "more of God" in your own home, every day. He came home from church with you last Sunday and He's still there, in your kitchen, bedroom and backyard.

> *Father, I ask You to meet me at home, on my commute or while the kids are napping. Help me to be mindful of You all week, to remember that You are here in my everyday comings and goings. I will watch for You and breathe in Your presence even now. Thanks, God. Amen*

seventeen

SITTING WITH JOYCE

THE FRONT OF THE large church sanctuary is crowded with people coming for prayer at the end of a beautiful service. The band plays softly. People are standing and worshiping along with the music. Many are kneeling as others pray for them.

I look around and wonder what I ought to do.

Should I go find someone to pray for?

As part of the large church staff, there is an understanding that we are there to minister to others whenever possible. But on this morning I do not really feel like moving from my seat on the front row next to my good friend, Joyce, another staff member who definitely lives up to the first three letters of her name.

Her eyes are closed and I can sense such a sweet peacefulness there that I wish we could just sit like this forever. Seriously. Stealing a glance at her, I see that tears are flowing silently down her cheeks.

I gently reach over and place my hand on her back. No words right now, not yet. I take a deep breath; the sweetness of God's presence is so real that I smile at a memory. I am thinking of a message I heard recently about "being out of our minds in love with God." It was based on Ephesians 3:18,19, where the apostle Paul prays that we would *"understand the love of Christ which passes understanding."*

> *..that Christ may dwell in your hearts through faith; that you, being grounded in love, may be able to comprehend... what is the width and length and depth and height...to know the love of Christ which passes knowledge; that you may be filled with the fullness of God.* Ephesians 3:17-19 NKJV

It sounds more than a little bit contradictory, doesn't it? This is why I am smiling as I ponder it. Ephesians is recording a prayer that we would be able to somehow grasp and understand the huge love of God. But right there in the same verse it states that this love is beyond our understanding! Hello?

The love of God is too big for our mind to comprehend. The only way to "get it" is to let go of the idea that our little minds can understand it. We can believe and know the love of God only by getting "out of our minds" and believing it. It is a spirit thing, not an intellectual thing, at times.

So, normally when I am in the situation of praying for someone, my mind is racing with inner questions. *Should I pray aloud so they can hear me? What should I be praying about? Maybe I ought to ask them what their need is. What are You doing God? What do You want me to say to her?*

But on this morning, sitting in the front row of a large church sanctuary, I relaxed and waited. I did not strive to figure out what God may be doing in Joyce or in me at that moment. I remembered the truth about being "out of my mind" and remained silent. I knew something was transferring from me to my friend and I just sat there with my hand on her back and enjoyed the peace of the moment.

Joyce and I probably sat like that for 10 or 15 minutes without a single word being spoken. I watched the people around us beginning to move about and do the normal after-church chatting and laughing. Lunch plans were being made, but I felt no desire to move out of our silent bubble of sweetness and rest. My eyes were open and I smiled at others, but did not want to talk to anyone just yet.

After about 15 minutes Joyce opened her eyes and looked at me. She softly spoke, *"Sooz, really good stuff was happening in me and you did not even need to "go there" with me verbally at all. Your presence truly carried me into God's presence. This atmosphere-changer thing is very real in you, Sooz."*

Her words brought tears to my eyes. Not only did my peaceful atmosphere affect my friend, but the words she spoke totally confirmed the silent prayer I had sent to God. I had asked Him if I needed to verbally pray for her and felt it was time to be quiet. I was blown away.

This is the power of His love. The love of God is an atmosphere changer. And we get to be the carriers of this amazing power. The power of His love can bring peace into a turbulent situation and rest to a struggling heart. When words will not do, a simple touch can make all the difference. It is beyond our understanding, this God-size love.

When Ephesians reminds us to seek to know the love of God, which is too much for us to understand, it is a call to get out of our minds. It is a challenge to those of us who tend to over-think and ultra-analyze our every waking moment. I do not have to feel peaceful in order to carry peace into a situation. My desire to have everything understood and figured out can hold me back from grasping His love because it is simply too big for me to comprehend.

If we wait until we can understand God's love, we will never be able to truly enjoy it and rest in it. This book is all about God's love for you and for me, but it is an inexhaustible subject—a limitless truth without boundaries or borders of any kind.

Sadly, many of us miss out on the fun of His love because we are using our heads to believe it. Remember the Ephesians passage?

His love will not fit in our heads.

It does not compute.

It makes no sense.

It is illogical.

We are to seek to know the love of God because He wants us to know Him better. His love is who He is. There is no separation between God and the love of God, it is not a part of Him, it IS Him.

God IS love.

YOUR TURN

God is in you, Dear One. You carry Him and so you are a carrier of His love. You are an atmosphere-changer. When you walk into a room, the love of God comes with you into that room.

Believe it.

Walk in that truth and watch the difference you can bring into a tough situation. Don't worry about finding the perfect words to speak. Do not strive to be the all-knowing wise counselor everywhere you go.

The beauty of this truth is that you will bring peace into a room without even working at it. You are a carrier. His spirit in you will change the atmosphere of a situation when you rest in Him.

Just BE the love carrier that God has designed you to be. That will be more than enough.

> *Thank You, Father, for choosing to use me as Your love-carrier and peace-bringer. Even when I do not feel perfectly peaceful, I know that You are big enough to enter a room with me and make a difference for everyone within my circle of influence. I am overwhelmed that You would do this through little old me. Thank You, Father! Amen*

eighteen

STOP READING AND START WRITING

MY LEGS AND BACK are beginning to feel numb from sitting on a thin carpet, laid over cold cement in the back room of my small town church in the middle of the day, in the middle of the week. I am surrounded by construction paper in yellow, red, green and black. Other items that litter the floor around me are yellow and black yarn, glitter, glue, scissors and a staple gun.

This description is just one moment out of innumerable happy experiences as the wife of the pastor in a very small church in a very small town. If you know anything about this unusual profession, you know that I was also…

- The church secretary
- The weekly bulletin writer and printer
- The Children's Church Director
- A Sunday School teacher
- The midweek Kids Club Leader
- The Women's Ministries Director
- The Co-Leader of the local Ministerial Wives monthly gathering
- A Christmas Pageant Director and costume maker
- A baby shower and wedding shower planner
- The church janitor
- An outreach coordinator
- A counselor
- A Kids Camp Coordinator and Counselor
- Other stuff that escapes me at the moment!

Hopefully you did not hear any self-pity or complaining in that list. If you did, it did not come from me. I loved it all. (Well, I did NOT love the janitorial bit!) The pastor's wife of a small town church does a lot of the work that would normally be parceled out to volunteers in a larger congregation. This is also true for the pastor of a small church, woman or man. I did not mind doing so much. To me it was a challenge and I made myself feel good by thinking that it was a useful way to make God proud of me. I loved the kids, the women and the way these tasks stretched me.

When I was spending my afternoons on the floor of the church fellowship hall, designing the children's church bulletin board, I was also singing along with worship music and praying for the kids in my care. I took this job and life-calling seriously. Yes, there were some days in my life as a pastor's wife that were definitely not full of singing and praying. On the hard days, if I was praying, it was more along these lines,

"How long, O Lord?"

I don't believe there are very many other professions where the wife of the person with the job title is so totally included in the duties of the job. The spouse of a church pastor is in a unique and challenging position. Some women have chosen it with strong intention. Others have been surprised to find themselves in such a spot. I wanted this job.

When I was a young pastor's wife I read book after book on the requirements and duties of my new position. Doing it right was my goal. I highlighted How-To books, took notes, and filled my journals with my mighty expectations. If there had been an actual book of rules for the wife of a pastor, I would have memorized it and carried reminder note cards in my purse.

Unfortunately, it was easy to find several books for ministry wives that sounded an awful lot like rule-books that could not be questioned. I devoured these flower-covered paperbacks until I became over-whelmed at what lay before me. I could not imagine myself accomplishing all that a good pastor's wife was meant to be.

For one thing, my quiet personality did not fit the out-going and *super*-talented women who were writing these books. I could not even play the piano. I complained to God that He might have made a mistake in choosing me for this job. Heaviness and fear threatened to paralyze me until I heard a small voice in my heart gently say,

"Daughter, stop reading."

It has been many years since that moment. But the journey of becoming a free woman in ministry has been and continues to be long and full of adventures, both wonderful and awful. I did stop reading those books on how to be a pastor's wife and now I have come to a place where I am hearing that same voice. But this time He is saying,

> ***"Talk to my Daughters…***
>
> ***Tell them that I am not as hard to please as they think I am."***

Was I working so hard in ministry to get God to like me? Was I adding up points so that He would be proud of me? I honestly do not think I would ever have stated it in that way. There are many ways to describe ministry jobs that sound much more noble and self-sacrificing than that. My heart was truly directed by a desire to please God.

What I did not realize years ago was that God was already entirely pleased with me. All those hours, days, months and years of serving Him as a church leader are beautiful and sweet to Him. But, they do not and did not affect His love for me one bit.

My Father's love and acceptance of me was complete from the beginning of time. He does not hold a scorecard, carefully adding up what I am doing or not doing for Him. He loved me as much when I was watching a movie as when I was teaching Sunday school. My hours on a cold cement floor preparing for children's church were precious to Him. But so were the days that I vegged out with a book in the backyard.

YOUR TURN

Friend, God is simply not as hard to please as you may think He is. If you are feeling over-whelmed today, let's look at what is weighing heaviest on you. Take a measure of the activities in your life.

Like cleaning out a closet, look at each thing and evaluate it's worth. Is it worth saving or is it something that can be let go? Ask yourself why you are doing that activity. Do you enjoy it? Does it make your heart sing? Are you working on that committee because you have been pressured to do so? Are you attending or leading that Bible study because it seems like the right thing to do?

This chapter has been about my early years in full-time ministry, so the examples have leaned heavily in that direction. But, all believers can be tempted to accept tasks, events and clubs with the unspoken idea that it will elevate them in God's eyes. Churches depend upon volunteers a great deal. When large groups of people work together, great things can happen that can change the world. We just have to be wary of our deepest motives when we raise our hand.

Keep in mind that God is not keeping a scorecard on you. Even if others are.

Most importantly, ask yourself if you are doing the thing in order to please God. It is certainly not wrong to desire to please God, but you need to know that He is already completely pleased and delighted with you. Right now, this moment God adores you and thinks you are the very best thing He ever created! When you wake up each morning, God knows that you both are beginning a brand new day together and He is thrilled about that!

If it is time for you to sit down with your calendar and delete some stuff, I am praying for you. My prayer is that God will highlight the items that need to go. I hope He will whisper to you about how much He would rather sit on the beach with you than on the back pew of another conference or meeting. You will know that He is crazy about you and He will help you give your calendar a ruthless diet.

> *Dear Father, I lift up my calendar to You. I hold up my long and complicated TO DO list and I ask You to please help me trim it down to size. Help me be strong in this process. Realign my thinking so that I am able to see my activities through Your gracious eyes. And I promise to cut what you say to cut. I promise to let go of the jobs I have taken on in order to make you love me more. Because Father, You already do love me more! Amen.*

nineteen

THE INSPIRATION

A YOUNG WOMAN WHOM I have never seen or spoken with in person sparked the beginnings of this book. She is a young ministry wife with small children and a pastor husband. Our connection happened online because we both write blogs. She enjoyed reading what I wrote and that led her to leave a few comments at the end of some of my blog posts. I began to read her blog and loved her sweet and spunky spirit. We are still friends more than 3 years later.

From the start I loved her enthusiasm and desire to be the very best pastor's wife and Christian mother that she can be. But when we first "met", her blog posts also sounded sad and frustrated because she was just trying so darn hard to be perfect for God. That is what pulled at my heart and actually made me a little bit angry.

I did not get mad at this young ministry wife. I got mad at the enemy for messing with her mind and the minds of many other young and old women who want so very much to be good enough for God and for their husbands. It stirred something up in me that has not lessened as the years have passed.

When I first began to write online, I researched other blogs that were labeled as “Christian”. I wanted to see what a believer’s blog is supposed to look and sound like. What I discovered was disheartening. At the time, there seemed to be two main styles of faith-driven blogs. There were the floral decorated devotional-style sites that were full of scripture and little mini-sermons. These revealed no personality or struggle from the writer.

The other style I found was overly strong, abrasive and political, with talk of spiritual warfare and victory over the world. Petitions and addresses for writing your congressmen filled the pages. There are readers for both of these styles, but I am not one of them.

So I decided to check out the personal blogs written by ministry wives and some well-known Christian women. Soon, I began to see a third trend that bothered me even more than the too-soft or too-hard versions already mentioned. My young friend was in this group. These were sincere believers who worked hard in their ministry and life but never felt as if they were doing enough. The sadness, tiredness and sense of hopelessness was sprinkled between the lines as they wrote about failing once again to get up an hour earlier each day to find some quiet time before the family woke up and “real life” began.

My new friend had three children under six at the time. She felt that she could not hear from God as well as her youth-pastor husband because she did not “spend as much time alone with God.” Somehow she had become subtly convinced that God’s love for her was measured by how much time she spent in prayer and service to Him.

I began to share with her some things I have learned and am still learning about the unconditional love of God that we ALREADY HAVE! He is already in love with us. Yes, we know that intellectually, and we even teach it in our church classes and Bible studies. But we do not live as if we believe it. I told her that she was already washing the dishes in God's presence. Folding laundry does not have to include loud worship music in order to make it a sweet moment with God. Her playtimes with the kids were worship to the Father God who gave them to her.

She told me that I was very wise and I should be writing about this truth more. I sat there with tears welling up, because I was not sure how to convey this truth. I do not know how to impart something that has taken me years to grasp and that I still question sometimes.

BUT, I do know this: I know, that I know, that I know, that God loves me. I have no doubts at all about His pleasure with me and His delight in me. Even today, when I am feeling shlumpy and kind of useless, my God loves me just as much today as He did when I was a pastor's wife and in charge of multiple committees and classes and ministries. JUST AS MUCH.

Maybe knowing that is enough for now.

> *"Yes, Jesus loves me.... "*

I have come full circle to the song I sang as a little girl. My online friend may be right about me, I am wise. It is the gleanings of a full life, combined with the wisdom of a child. The Jesus Loves Me song is the first song we learn in church as little kids. It is the basic truth. It is the simple truth. And I choose to believe it.

YOUR TURN

Dear One, you are loved today just as much as you will be when you have completed all the great goals you have set up for yourself.

Guilt is not your friend.

You know that already.

But did you know that God does not use guilt to get us to change our ways? It does not work. Not for long anyway. If you feel guilty about your lack of spiritual discipline, it could be time to take another look at what you consider important to your relationship with God.

You may have been taught that the Bible reading chart is vital to your ability to hear from God. I would heartily agree that God loves to speak to us through His beautiful Word…but He is ALWAYS talking in a myriad of other forms also. The sky, the animals and the people around us are all messages from His heart to ours. Do not allow guilt about the lack of check marks on a Bible reading chart keep you from listening and enjoying The Father who already loves you completely and is speaking sweet nothings in your ear.

God loves you in the same measure that He loves the most sacrificial missionary. It is a difficult thing to believe, but it is true. He loves differently than we love. Ours can grow, change and disappear. God is love. His entire being is all about love. You no longer need to strive to be worthy of His love.

You already are.

Father, it really is hard for me to understand that You can love me, as I am, in this moment and this day. Can You help me switch off the desire to strive for what I already have? Will you elevate my desire for you? Thank You for loving me. Thank You for knowing me and still loving me right now, in this moment. Amen.

twenty

THE TIME GOD CAUGHT ME FLUFFING MY HAIR

I REACHED BACK TO fluff my hair. When you have thin, fine hair, a great deal of energy goes into adding fullness in any way you are able. I had been sitting on the floor with my head leaned back against the wall in our ministry school worship room.

As soon as I did it, I talked to myself. And then God talked to me.

I immediately and sternly scolded myself for being so vain. After all, who worries about their hair while they are PRAYING? I berated myself for being so shallow and I looked around to see who might have seen me fluffing my hair. This was followed by yet another reprimand for caring what others think.

This is when I distinctly heard God say to my spirit,

> ***"What if NOTHING you did was wrong? Why don't you experiment with that thought a bit?"***
>
> *EXCUSE me?*

What if God looks at us like an adoring new parent looks at their baby?

I am a new grandparent, but I have a lot of friends who are in the young parenting stage. This means that my social media feed is often full of baby pictures and videos. These mommies and daddies are so proud of their babies... just for being born. The baby is a drooling, wobbly, burping blob of humanity, and the new parents are enthralled.

I watched one video of a newborn yesterday titled something along the lines of "Cute Breathing". The baby was sound asleep and we all got to watch and listen to her breathing. Breathing! I kept watching in case something funny was going to happen at the end… nope, just breathing!

I will not tell you how many times I have watched the latest video of my grandson learning to crawl. My clicks alone may cause that video to go viral.

Can you play with the idea that God is just as entranced with you? That He is simply so in love with you that you can do no wrong? I KNOW! That is a crazy ridiculous thought. But experiment with it a bit.

What if God's love for you is bigger than your mess-ups? What if He watched you fail at something and in His eyes it was just a baby burp? It was a bit of drool sliding down your chin? Is He going to yell at you with impatience as you attempt to take a few steps, but land on your behind?

Of course, we need to mature beyond the baby steps. We grow and learn to control our burps (Well, most of us do.) But I am convinced that God's love for us is bigger than our capacity to fail. How big is that? Our ability to mess up is ridiculously huge. Right? We make mistakes on a grand scale... daily.

But God is bigger.

I used to worry about accidental sin. I would not walk through the atheist section of the bookstore. I refused to enter little gift shops that sold crystals and incense. I would not even watch the television show, "The Big Bang Theory" because the title sounded like it was about evolution. (All clear signs of some serious Church Lady Syndrome by the way.)

I was afraid of falling away from God.

Accidentally.

As if that is easy to do. Then one day I saw a picture in my mind of God's hands. They were gigantic. His hands were bigger than the universe, wider than could be seen. And there I was in the middle of God's mighty hands, so tiny. How could I ever get all the way to the edge and fall away? It would have to be entirely intentional. Even then, I could imagine His fingers curling up a bit, just enough to keep me inside the safety of His hands. Falling away from God would not be easy or accidental.

His love for me and for you is full of eternity's patience.

What if you could do no wrong in His eyes? What if He never hangs His head in shame or disappointment with you? What if every thought of you brings a crazy-big smile to His face? I know that these "what ifs" may be difficult to believe.

But there is a problem with our tendency to believe that God may be upset with us. It keeps us from looking up at Him in confidence. When you feel you have wronged someone, what do you do when they come near? You look down and avoid them.

You make excuses to stay away from them.

When we think that we have disappointed God, it sets up a barrier between Him and us. We feel ashamed and do not feel worthy to be near Him. So He comes close and whispers love words to us and we shut them down and proceed to spill out our repentance and regret for all the sins we've ever done or thought about doing. We try to get cleaned up before entering His presence. Or we simply stay away from Him and begin to build up a wall to keep Him away. We want to get cleaned up before facing Him.

While we are blubbering on about our awfulness, He is standing there with wide-open arms, ready to make it all better.

YOUR TURN

In this chapter I have asked you to compare the love that God has for us to the unabashed love that a new parent has for their baby. But even human parents fall short of this high standard of love. Earthly fathers and mothers can sometimes feel embarrassed or ashamed of their children's actions. God's love goes far beyond our human capacity to love. His love is unconditional. His love is not based on His reputation or how well we obey Him. Yes, we will have to endure the consequences of intentional sin against Him, but His love for us will not be altered by our actions.

You give Him pleasure just by breathing. Your existence is a delight to God. Simply by being alive.

When the Ruler of The Universe looks at you, it is with the adoring eyes of a new parent. You can do no wrong in those eyes.

"Look, she burped... isn't that the cutest thing?"

"There she goes, fluffing her hair again."

> *Father, thank You for loving me simply because I am alive. I do not want to have any walls between us. So today I believe that You love me unconditionally and without reserve. I am grabbing on to that truth and looking full into Your face with confidence in the love You have for me. You love me. Thank you! Amen.*

twenty-one

YOUR FAT IS BEAUTIFUL

WHEN WE LIVED IN CALIFORNIA my husband and I loved our weekends on his motorcycle, flying around our picturesque country roads. The freedom of getting out of the house and enjoying the beauty of God's creation always gave me a sense that all was right in my world. It was also full of delight because I could forget about the dishes in the sink and the laundry that needed folding back at the house.

As I sat behind my husband, I often found myself smiling and worshiping God as we pointed out the beautiful sights we were always discovering in our area. I talked to God and thanked Him for His goodness to us.

One day while we roamed the countryside, I heard a very quick and clear sentence from God that messed me up a lot. I was wearing a black tank top, covered up by a black button down shirt. The wind had pulled the shirt back to reveal my tank-covered tummy.

When I looked down, I grimaced at the ugly rolls of belly fat that I saw. I immediately "heard" God say to me,

> ***"Your fat is beautiful."***

> *What?*

Let me say right here, that even a husband knows never to say such a thing to his wife.

A careful husband might say, *"I love the way you look"* or *"You are perfect just the way you are"* or any number of similar versions that will keep him out of trouble and still be close to honest. But a smart man will never say what God had just said to me!

God told me that my fat is beautiful. What in the world do I do with this information? Many of my friends are hearing God talk to them. He is telling them how to transform a nation. He is giving them vision plans for feeding the poor, and helping them create strategies that will stop the sex slave industry.

My God tells me that my fat is beautiful.

I still do not know why God gave me such an odd message. It did not get shared to our church the following Sunday, that's for sure. It was our little secret.

But this shocking sentence reminded me once again that God is very different from us. His view and His values are galaxies away from mine. You know that verse about how God's thoughts are not our thoughts? (Isaiah 55:8) So true! God has a completely different measuring tape for life.

My God who loves me, even adores me, looks at me and sees beauty. He does not see the failure or the extra fat that is so obvious to me. He also does not equate fat with failure, as I do. I cannot help but compare myself to society's beauty standard. Which is pretty silly because recently, even society is recognizing how unrealistically Hollywood and the modeling world has portrayed women and their bodies.

My wonderful God is messing up my mind with surprising sentences like this—words that are revealing who He is. He is giving me little clues about His character and His ways. I do not understand the concept of calling rolls of fat beautiful. I also cannot say I agree with Him on this just yet. Let's say that we are working on this one together.

But I can try to stop frowning at myself so much. I can stop grumbling at the parts of my body that do not measure up to society's odd standards. My words to myself need to match His. My self-talk needs to be full of kindness and as much grace as I offer to others so freely. If I have asked God to live in me, to live in my mind, my heart and my body, then frowning at the mirror is not something I want to be doing, is it?

YOUR TURN

Dear Friend, look at yourself. Look at your body, your face and hair. Do you release a sigh of frustration? Maybe you don't. We all have the "good" days and the "ugly" days. I can love my hair one day and hate it the next.

Embrace who you are in your body today. Decide today that you will not allow current fashion to determine how you feel about your own body. The culture of fashion changes constantly. Put Marilyn Monroe next to Twiggy and see how silly it would be to judge yourself by fashion's slippery standards. God loves you and your belly. He adores your nose. He likes your freckles.

His love is pure. It is beyond our imagination. God's love for you is so complete that He lets out a sigh when He looks at you. But it is not a sigh of sadness or disgust. It is a sigh of adoration and enchantment. He smiles at every thought of you and those thoughts add up to more than the grains of sand on all the beaches in the world.

> *Thank You, Father, for loving my fat. I do not understand it, but I accept it and will try to embrace this body You have given me. You live in me, so how could I be mean or cruel to Your dwelling place? Thank You, God, for my body. Amen.*

twenty-two

YOUR FRIENDSHIP WITH JESUS

I AM GOING TO MAKE a statement that will not shock or surprise you in any way.

> *Your friendship with God is more important than your ministry.*

I know! Big deal, right? Of course, you and I know this. After all, which came first, your relationship with The Father or your ministry? (Actually, the answer to that one COULD very well complicate things a bit with some.) But for most of us, we fell in love with God and our deep love and dedication to His Son led us into a life of ministry, either volunteer or vocationally. Our desire to share that love with others led to ministry jobs, outreaches and activities that gave us a way to "spread the good news".

The complication that slips into our lives later, is that our busy-ness doing His business slowly starts to creep into our intimate time with Him. You know what I mean don't you? You finally grab a moment to just sit and breathe and be still with God, and the long to-do list for the upcoming women's luncheon pops into your mind. You volunteered to help out at Vacation Bible School all summer. Or the notes for the Bible study need to be copied off, the nursery needs re-organizing, the Fall Retreat is still missing a driver, and the conference next month still needs tweaking!

Yikes, just writing all of that made me jumpy and nervous!

It is understandable and acceptable for some crazy-busy weeks to happen a few times a year. These are seasonal. The "Holidays" are notorious for being anything but merry for those in ministry jobs. Sometimes church or ministry organization events will cause our lives to slip into chaos-mode for a week or two. I believe that is normal and to be expected.

BUT…

A stressful schedule that has become the norm is a danger signal. Exhaustion is not pleasing to The Father's heart. It is not. He is more concerned with YOU. An over-loaded life happens when we fall into the habit of taking on more jobs than we can handle. If we are slipping into a pattern of accepting jobs or responsibilities because "if I don't do it, it won't get done," we are entering a really dangerous place to live.

I have had to learn that my relationship with Jesus is number one. My friendship with Jesus is number one. My romance with Jesus is

NUMBER ONE. If my time is filled to overflowing with ministry events and planning, I start to sense a hunger that is not being fed. I don't even know what is missing at first! Sometimes it is hard to recognize what is wrong with this picture. Life is good, people are being healed, hurting people are being set free and we are getting it done!

But the thought comes… *God, are You there? Hellooo?*

My message to you is a simple one. But it is often difficult to carry out. Say that little two-letter word a bit more often. You know the one…"No."

But, but, but! Yes, I know all the "buts" and "what ifs." And to your questions and protestations I ask another question...

> *Which came first?*
>
> *Who comes first?*
>
> *He loves WHO you are much more than what you DO.*

YOUR TURN

If your love affair with Jesus has dimmed, it could be due to working too hard for Him.

Look at your schedule objectively. I suggest listing the jobs that you are involved in and putting a little heart next to the tasks that you enjoy. The chores that are heartless will include some essentials, but you may discover a few that can be deleted from your life.

Are you attending a Bible study group that no longer interests you, but you feel obligated to be involved? Did you step in and volunteer to oversee a church event that you are tired of? Does stress build up in you when you think about an upcoming committee meeting? It is possible that these are your "heartless" jobs and it is time to re-evaluate your involvement.

Believe it or not, there are others who may be waiting in the wings to oversee these tasks with joy and excitement. Step aside and allow someone else to fill that need. The peace you experience will be worth the temporary guilt. Your love affair with Jesus is more important than your to-do list. He is not lying awake at night, wringing his hands over who will organize the next teachers' meeting.

You are number one on His list of priorities. Being with you is number one on His to-do list.

Be there.

Father, You are number one in my heart and I want You to be number one in my daily life. If I have allowed my work FOR You to replace my relationship WITH You, I ask Your forgiveness. I ask You to help me change direction and reset my priorities. I love You and I now move You to the very first position in my priority list. The rest will fall into the proper spots once You are in the number one spot. Thank You, Father. Amen.

twenty-three

WHEN GOD THINKS OF YOU

FRIEND, WE ARE NEARING the end of this little book. I hope that the stories of my personal encounters with God have impacted you and helped you to believe how much He loves you.

I am not extraordinary or unusual in any aspect; I am you, a beloved child of God.

Now I have a fun interactive challenge for you. Are you ready for some participation? This was one of my favorite activities to do with the students in our small ministry school. The following statements must be read ALOUD.

You can do it in a room alone or find a small group and do it together. Either way, it is guaranteed to be a powerful act. I wrote these statements from real life experience and I too, have trouble believing them sometimes. But I still know them to be true.

Faith must be engaged when we struggle to accept how much God loves us. Verbalizing His love for us is a healthy way to move from hope, to faith, to real belief. When we speak these affirmations to ourselves, about ourselves, it changes the way we think and believe.

My favorite style of using this little activation is to print each sentence out on a separate slip of paper and hand them out randomly to a group. I usually number them so they are read in this order, even though they are handed out randomly. Every time I have done this activity with a group of people, it brought up powerful emotions. There have been awkward silences, tears and laughter as each one struggled to read the words before them. The beauty of handing the sentences out randomly is that I believe and I try to help the readers believe, that it is not truly "random". Holy Spirit knows who needs to read each statement, and He sets us up perfectly every time.

Yes these sentences must be spoken aloud. It makes a difference, you'll see. Try not to argue with or skip any of these facts. Ready, set, go!

- When God thinks of me, He smiles!
- When God hears my voice addressing Him, He leans forward and listens as if I am the most important voice in the universe.
- God looks forward to our times together with anticipation.
- If I miss some appointments with God, He still greets me with total joy and acceptance the next time!
- God actually takes delight in me!
- He knows my deepest, most secret thoughts and they do not

weaken His delight in me one bit.

- God winces with pain when I put myself down.
- God speaks words of encouragement to me through the people who love me.
- The words of disappointment and condemnation that I sometimes hear are never from Him.
- He looks for ways to protect me and give me joy.
- He may even chuckle when He steps in to protect me from danger and I never even know it.
- God loves to surprise me with good things.
- God loves my unique song.
- I can do nothing to change God's love for me.
- I am His prized possession.
- He cannot take His eyes off me.
- God says that I am a sweet aroma to Him.
- That's why He loves to be close to me.
- I am my Beloved's and He is mine.
- I am SO God's favorite!

There is power in truth. Everything in you will want to argue with these statements. You will want to add a "but..." to the end of each one. Stop yourself from arguing with the truth of His love for you. You will not win that argument. God has a pretty powerful case and He does not give up... ever.

You might as well surrender now.

Believe that the one and only Creator of The Universe loves you.

You are SO His favorite! Got it?

twenty-four

THE *HOW-TO* CHAPTER

DEAR FRIEND, YOU HAVE OBVIOUSLY seen by now that this book has a singular message. It has been stated more times than I can count. In every conceivable way that I can say it to you. I have said it in stories, in my own personal "Ah ha" moments, in quiet conversations with God, and in chuckles between God and me.

GOD LOVES YOU,

COMPLETELY

AND WITHOUT RESERVE

TODAY.

But you may still be wondering how to grab this truth once and for all. You might be worried that once you close the last page of this book, all of the good feelings that came with it will slip away. That all the strong confidence in how much God loves you will wither away and you will be back where you started.

Before I share my "How To" advice, I want to tell you that there is no "once and for all" method. Believing that God loves you unconditionally is an ongoing battle every single day. We have an enemy who is working very hard to steal that truth from us. Because living in the love of God is more powerful than you know. It is your weapon. Your deep belief in God's love for you is in fact, your strongest weapon.

It can also be your life jacket. After more than 25 years in fulltime vocational ministry alongside my husband, we hit a painful roadblock a few years ago that shook my identity to the core. Several big life changes happened at once and I found myself stripped of job, ministry, friendships and home. Two close family deaths and a serious motorcycle accident in our family added to the pain and sense of deep loss.

During that difficult season I wrote the following conclusions on my blog.

> *WHAT I KNOW FOR SURE...*
>
> *In this time of transition and shift in my life, I am dropping off old beliefs, examining new thoughts and ideas, re-evaluating old mindsets and thought habits, both positive and negative. I am holding long-held truths up to the light and squinting my eyes to see if I believe them anymore.*

What I still believe is kept, and what I am no longer sure of gets set aside for closer examination. I am asking myself the hard questions of "Do I think this way because I never really considered any other?" and "Has that value I tried to live out, really worked or not?"

Digging down to the rock bottom foundation of what I believe and do not believe is extremely personal and sometimes painful. I still do not want to admit even the tiniest kernel of doubt about my faith in God...because it is just super scary! I am guilty of doing what that song in that Mormon Musical on Broadway says, "They just believe!" Insinuating that they do not think or examine, they just believe. But I have been thinking, examining and questioning.

Turns out, I am still completely in love with God and I am convinced that He still loves me. The deepest darkest questions have led me right back to knowing that God is good and that Jesus is real and worth my worship and trust. There will always be an element of faith, a piece of belief that cannot be scientifically or comprehensively explained and charted out for others to understand and grasp.

I think that maybe God likes it that way.

Some things that I know are true:

God loves me.

God loves you.

God wants me to love you.

God is good, and just because I cannot explain why awful stuff happens, it does not change this fact.

I gain strength and peace when I worship God.

I also gain strength and peace when I get mad at him. He is ok with that.

> God smiles at me and wants me to smile back.
>
> I am not too old to learn new thoughts and ideas about Him.
>
> I will never get to the end of all there is to know and discover about God.

I think that if you begin to look at what you believe, you will see that it is surprisingly difficult to get past the jargon, Bible stories, and traditional church phraseology that first come to mind. The truth is there, it is in you, but until you dig it out for yourself and hold it up to the light and see it with your own squinty eye, it will be a borrowed truth, not your own. Now I am back to more digging, questioning and experimenting.

During that rough time in my life, I was forced to come back to the basics. Ministry, job, friends and home were stripped away and I was left with only one real truth… **God loves me**. I am now walking out the lessons that my husband and I taught our ministry school students and church congregations for so many years. God is not measuring out His love for me according to my jobs and successful projects. God loves me today, just as I am. Even though I am between churches and will be listening to worship music on my couch next Sunday.

Still, it is an ongoing and continuous battle. The other night I was kept awake for several hours worrying about an issue in my life that is so small, so ridiculously unimportant. But instead of grabbing on to the love of God and how much He cares about every little part of my life, I lay there and worried myself into a sleepless knot. The battle to keep myself in the love of God is relentless.

But there are some shortcuts and helpful pathways that make it a quicker fight than it used to be.

Here's a little word-picture that God showed me. I hope it will help you too.

The vacant field about three blocks from my house was a popular shortcut to my school when I was a kid. Dividing the weed-covered square into two triangles, a path went from corner to corner. It was gouged with evidence of bikes riding through wet mud. Later, after being hardened by the sun, the deep grooves became permanent ruts from one corner of the field to the other.

I picture that rutted path now when I catch myself slipping into the old default place of fearful thinking. We know that scientists have found that we have brain pathways; thinking patterns set in place by habits and repetition. The patterns or pathways in your brain took years to form. It will require an intentional effort to change the habit and discover a new pathway of thinking.

But it can be done. You can be the BOSS of your brain.

Imagine yourself on a bike and your wheels are stuck in one of those deep ruts. What has to happen to release your bike from the deep ridge of dirt? Continuing your ride and simply turning your wheel is not going to work. It would be easier to just stay in the rut and go where you've always gone before. Using the path of least resistance. At least you will go to a familiar place.

But what if you want to go somewhere new?

It is going to take some determined action to release you from the old pathway.

Romans 8:5, 6 give us a clue to escaping the rut.

> *For those who live according to the flesh set their minds on the flesh, but those who live according to the spirit, the things of the spirit… to be spiritually minded is life and peace.* NKJV

According to this passage found in Romans, we can *"set our minds"*, or choose where we will allow our thoughts to linger, or meditate.

I had to learn how to stop my bike, or my fearful thought, and pull myself up and out of the rut. 2 Corinthians 10: 3-5 states,

> *Though we walk in the flesh, we do not war according to the flesh. The weapons of our warfare are not carnal but mighty in God for pulling down strongholds, casting down arguments and everything that exalts itself against the knowledge of God, bringing every thought into captivity to the obedience of Christ.* NKJV

Our negative, fearful thoughts could be described as "strongholds, arguments and everything that exalts itself against the knowledge of God." The key to changing our thinking patterns from negative to positive is to take our thoughts captive.

While writing this book, I had to intentionally "put my feet down and stop my bike" to change the pathway of my thinking. Negative circumstances had made me begin to question this crazy idea of writing a book. Who do I think I am anyway? I am no authority on anything. I felt down, depressed and naïve. I did not see a strong and confident woman in the mirror, so why would I think anyone would want to read what I had to say?

Such a train of thought can only lead to depression and the belief that I have nothing to offer. These thoughts can begin to spiral down and the layers of negativity begin to sound true and familiar. I want to repeat that: the negative thoughts sound true and familiar. My old brain patterns are still there. They are a default that I can slip into easily. It is so simple to just stay there, because it is familiar and comfortable. The temptation to wallow a bit is real. But worry is actually just negative meditation.

I saw what was happening and recognized the old thought pattern and it made me angry. Angry at the lies and determined not to stay in the ugly rut of negativity one minute longer. Walking in the love of God sharpens my awareness of what is true and what is a lie. Jude 20 reminds us to be…

> *Building yourselves up on your most holy faith, praying in the Holy Spirit,* ***keep yourselves in the love of God,*** *looking for the mercy of our Lord Jesus Christ unto eternal life.* Jude 20, 21 NKJV

We cannot will ourselves to think happy thoughts, but we can use our will to get to our spirit.

I shifted my thoughts away from my faults and inadequacies and onto the love of God. I reminded myself of all the ways God has told me He loves me, as described in this little book. I "pulled up" and out of the old default rut by reminding myself of the love of God. My bike was not allowed to stay on the old pathway.

Speaking of pathways, let's leave the rutted bike path and return to the silly little butterfly in her matching shoes and purse.

Do you see her walking along the sidewalk?

The butterfly was walking because she believed that she still had a lot of work to do to be qualified to fly. But she was wrong. She has a pair of gorgeous and colorful wings on her back and it is beyond time for her to stop dragging them behind her. It is time to let them unfurl and lift her up higher than she's ever been. I see those wings as the amazing and ridiculous love of God. His love is right there! Ready to lift her up… up… up!

There is no clear path up there, but **The Creator of The Universe LOVES HER… so it is time to fly!**

YOUR TURN

Do you want to live in the love of God? What does that even mean? Living in the love of God means that even when God seems to be playing hide & seek with you and He is being quiet, you wrap yourself up in the knowledge that He loves you completely. Period. The end. You are bravely choosing to be the boss of your brain. You can do this. Read on for a few practical steps to trick yourself back into peace.

When you find yourself dwelling on the negative issues in your life, (and we all have them) it is time to make a decision. It is not an easy decision. This can happen in a split second. You might be comfortable with spending hours, days or months in a downward spiral of negativity. But if you are sick and tired of being depressed and cranky about your life, there are some ways to pull up and out of the down hill journey. (Clinical depression requires a doctor's advice, but these ideas will not hurt along the way.)

This first step will sound shallow and cliché, but it works. Find your happy place. The love of God. Do whatever it takes to get there.

Does music move you? Make yourself turn on some music that is the opposite of your bad mood. It will feel odd and may even feel silly or manipulative, but do it anyway. There are no rules against manipulating yourself. You go to work to gain money, you fix your hair in order to feel better, why not give as much attention to lifting your mood and changing your mindset?

Use Scripture to change your thoughts if that is what helps you. Declare a promise out loud that God has given you. Pray in the Spirit, do a dance or get some physical exercise to jolt you out of the downward spin that negative thinking will take you. Print out some reminders from this book and keep them in front of you until the truth becomes your own.

Get together with other people. Negative thinking is a private and dangerously inward place to dwell. Find someone to talk to about your struggles. Trusted friends will give you another viewpoint and you will feel the heaviness lift just by sharing your thoughts.

Taking our thoughts captive requires strength and determination. It can be a little bit like trying to keep a dozen kittens inside a box with no lid. As you are grabbing one, another will escape. As quickly as one takes off, pull it back where it belongs. It takes constant surveillance and purpose. But if we can create a new pathway of freedom, it is worth the work.

Simply banishing the dark thought is not enough though. It must be replaced. The space will not remain empty.

What better replacement than the magnificent love of God? His love for you can fill every need, every want and every missing piece in your life. Talk to yourself about how much God loves you. He will join the conversation, because He started it, deep inside your spirit. His Spirit in you is constantly speaking to your spirit, and I believe that you can get in on that holy discussion. The more often you join that conversation, the easier it is to see the new pathway clearly.

Jude 20 reminds us to **keep ourselves in the love of God**. I find it interesting that we are given this assignment, don't you? The love of God is right there for us. No one else can provide it. You have it. Your wings are right behind you. You are carrying some big wings that are designed to carry you.

Dear One, The Creator of the Universe adores you. Today… As is… In this moment. It is time to let your wings lift you up. Let His love lift you into brand new places of wonder.

Father, I come to You with my hands on the handlebars of my bike and I am stopping and intentionally pulling the bike out of my old rut of worry and fear.

I want to explore Your new pathways that lead to peace and joy. I may not like the unknown, but YOU KNOW, so I can trust You today. I place my trust in Your love that passes understanding. Your love is trustworthy. Your love is beyond my imagination. Your love is my happy place!

Thank You Father God, for loving me the way You do! Thank you for teaching me how to FLY! Amen.

ABOUT THE AUTHOR

SUSIE KLEIN worked alongside her husband Curt for over 30 years in California while raising two sons. First they sold shoes together, and then, as he was a youth pastor, associate pastor, and pastor. Together they also founded and were Overseers of an adult ministry school that still gives them great pleasure as they keep up with their former students all over the world.

Susie and her husband now live in Texas, near her eldest son, his adorable wife and magnificent grandson. Part of her heart is still in California with her creative younger son.

She is a freelance writer and professional blogger for online businesses. But her favorite cyber-spot is her own blog, Recovering Church Lady.

Resources

Susie's Blog: recoveringchurchlady.com

Freelance Writer Website: www.SusieKlein.wordpress.com

The book *Walking Butterfly* is available online in paperback at www.amazon.com

30734424R00089

Made in the USA
San Bernardino, CA
21 February 2016